THE DRAGON'S TOOTH

[An Original Practice fantasy play in 3 acts.]

The Dragon's Tooth

[*An Original Practice fantasy play in three acts.*]

by

J.L. Davis

Characters

[In order of appearance.]

Melsyne-A Sword Maiden of Natiro.
Drond-A Famed Warrior of Natiro.
Quik-Granddaughter to Drond, sister to Melsyne.
Rykel-An unscrupulous man.
Ekinroy-A Knight of North Kalas.
Wizard-A faceless traitor.
Bazeen-A Wizard's Champion.
Bandit #1.
Bandit #2.
Bandit #3.
Crier.
Citizen #1.
Citizen #2.
Cragmyre-King of North Kalas.
Royal Guard #1.
Royal Guard #2.
Gwendolyn-Betrothed of Ekinroy.
Sir Gyle-Friend or Ekinroy.
Merchant-An unlawful trader known by many names.
Medias-A mender.
Loren-A young Mender in training.
Whorlick-A dirty hireling.
Blart-A filthy hireling.
Mercenary Captain.
Mercenaries.
Ferryperson #1.
Ferryperson #2.

*All performers except the leads should play multiple characters.

*This play is written to be performed outdoor or indoor on scrolls with a single text session and minimal group rehearsals (Original Practice Shakespeare style), OR fully produced per modern standards.

*Original Practice Guidelines and General Notes are provided at the end of the script for any who wish to reference them.

Act I, Scene 1
[Enter Melsyne, Drond, Quik.]

Mel. This mountain air, immaculate to breathe might leave one wond'ring why tales make it seem that so unseemly, teeming with malfeasance and indecency, the land around is quite so mean as some would have those from our island home believe.

Dro. Believe Melsyne, for I have seen much more than thee. The land makes not the man in these unmannerly amoral mainland nations. All thieves and whores no more acquainted with a proper occupation than a salty crocodile with communication.

Mel. Grandfather-

Quik *[Chanted.]*

> *(How many whores per corner*
> *could a crooked kingdom sport?*
> *A score of whores per acre*
> *or a hundred whores per court!)*

Mel. Let's not forget we travel in the presence of a child.

Quik I am no child *Melsyne*!

Mel. Yes *Quik*, you are to me.

Quik But I just turned fourteen.

Mel. I know thy age as well as thee, for I help'd change thy swaddle-ing.

Quik Gross.

Mel. Our childhood ends not when we some arbitrary number reach, but rather when we're wise enough that we ourselves have lessons we may teach.

Quik Well I just help'd our grandfather solve a mathematical equation.

Dro. Thy sister, though she does not elevate the conversation, correctly calculates the local concentration. The cutthroats hereabout concern me even more.

Quik How does one quantify the diff'rence in the danger 'tween a cutthroat and-

Mel. How fortunate to have a famed warrior with us then. Thy very name grandfather does deter unsav'ry men. ('That *Drondstaff* didst thou say who near three decades did defend us all upon that darkest day? When demons from across the Split spill'd forth, that very *Drond* did block their way?')

Quik ('The aged hero from Natiro'?)

Mel. ('Whose bladed staff did route the floods however rough, his sturdy frame a formidable bulwark when-)

Dro. Enough, enough. Tis true we're not defenseless lambs, yet ambling through this foreign land unwarily can only lead to ill. We all must careful tread with each our head upon a swivel, keeping conversation quiet short and simple.

Quik Then I shall walk as wary as a harlot through a temple.

Mel. Quik-

Quik I said harlot.

Mel. Dost thou know even what such slanders mean?

Quik Not precisely no, (although a book I've seen kept commonly by bedside counters includes 'whore' some thirty times or more in five translations.)

Mel. Such books be writ by men that they might justify their domination of contrary populations, (and should not be prescrib'd to those unwise enough to recognize a metaphor or moral bas'd manipulation.) Let keep us moving that we may camp near the mountain's peak, and on the morning reach the dreaded dragon den we seek.

[Exeunt.]

[Enter Rykel.]

Ryk. *[Mostly sung.]*

> *(There was a most valiant young knight,*
> *who knew not the feeling of fright,*
> *when he went to slay the dragon.*
> *He kill'd the abhorred ol' drake,*
> *such a surly and slipp'ry snake,*
> *but the knight he ain't a' braggin'.*

Ha, why? you ask, and I'm so glad you did, oh most inquisitive inventions of my own imagination. A lengthy story un-elongated: because he too is dead; hee-hee-hee! A toast to temp'ral liberation, a very unequivocal occasion for libation; so long as thou are not the one on permanent vacation. *[Drinks.]* Ah.

> *The blade slid in the leath'ry skin,*
> *by all accounts the knight did win,*
> *alive by the skin of his teeth.*
> *But he'll never come home,*
> *to that great golden dome,*
> *for the knight is now trapped underneath!*

Hee-hee-hee-heeeeeee; what seems to be the trouble master? So sorry but your words are muffl'd. Methinks you speak of some unspeakable disaster? You're asking me to help you with some weighty matter? You know that I am but a lowly squire, only hi-r'd out of pious mercy. And so, good sir, I am unworthy; and pray you rot most nob-l-y.

> *I could have tried to intercede,*

But then, I'm filled with greed,
So I left him right there it's the truth.
Then I cut the thing free,
Now it belongs to me,
You see I, remov'd the dragon's tooth.

And soon I will be very, very, rich.)
[Enter Drond.]

Who slithers up on me unknown?
Dro. A weary trav'ler, far from home.
Ryk. But brigands beasts and burly brutes traverse these mountain, routes, old man.
Dro. And which of those are you then?
Ryk. A trav'ling minstrel friend; yes that is what I am.
Dro. Then that was your voice croaking as a toxic toad had chose this wood to end his tortur'd lifely woes?
Ryk. An aging gentleman alone would wisely watch his tongue if he had hopes to one day see again his home.
[Enter Melsyne, Quik.]

How very nice, you've brought the fam'ly to this frontier far from paradise.
Mel. The three of us hail from Natiro, and so fear we nothing in these unfamiliar lands. His name is *Drond*, and there is strength left in those weather'd hands.
Ryk. None but a fool would seek to duel with father time. I've heard the young and old of your Natiro fight beside men in their prime.
Mel. As do we women, test me if you dare.
Ryk. A woman say you? Barely there, though one might be persuaded were thy adm'rable anatomy laid bare.
Mel. My steel is all I'll bare; and pray you never see the glint of it descending t'ward you or your intimates. I nothing am a fawning maiden of your land, who hides a

painted face behind a silken fan in some anticipation of attracting an unwary wealthy man. I hear that fierceness here is found to be unfeminine, and free will in a woman an impediment, but many women in the marshes train their martial skills to soldierly precision, indiff'rent of such simple-minded sentiment. You look upon a warrior of the marsh, battle-tested in the harsh conditions of the Split, my body hon'd for battle in this world, my spirit strong for combat that comes after it.

Ryk. (*Disdainful for a gangly girl*.) Apologies oh mighty maiden, there's more sense I'd say in softening thy slender form that some young fellow find it more, appealing. The rest is cause for mirth, for what a waste to wage a war on nothing, hee-heeee.

Mel. The cheapest form of ridicule is laughter. When words and wisdom fail, like gas'ous bubbles in the swamp it rises to the surface after. The nature of mortality is such that we may nothing know what lies beyond the veil, so lack of preparation for a struggle is but setting thyself up to fail. Just as the challenges endur'd in youth prepare us for the greatest earthly foes; or for the most, uncouth.

Ryk. So sage for one so young, and what a tongue, but words will not lay down with thee upon a cold and lonely night.

Mel. My worth lies less within a lie, and more inside a fight.

Ryk. Diversionary tactics?

Quik Melsyne could whip a wimp like you before she lost a baby tooth.

Ryk. Forgive me little whelp, I could not help forget thou dawdling down there in the denser air.

Quik (Now that was most unfair). This whelp herself would whoop your derriere. Unfortunately I don't have the time to take such sport, for we are on a quest of great import.

Mel. Quik-

Ryk. What secret quest could cause a brittle bird to herd his hatchlings so far from their wat'ry nest?

Dro. Our bus'ness is our own.

Quik We've come to call the dragon from his home.

Ryk. So drastic is the difference in height, I'm sure I didn't hear thee right.

Quik WE-HAVE-COME-TO-SPEAK-WITH-THE-DRAGON-YOU-GANGLY-WASTE OF SLIGHTLY ELEVATED OXYGEN.

Ryk. Thou've come to Speak with mighty Monwyrm, and expect that you will not be burn'd? Hee-hee-hee-heeee, (I've stumbl'd on the missing dodo and his clutch. I don't believe I've ever laugh'd so much, or heard of birds so firmly out of touch.)

Quik He'll speak with us regardless of his might, and when we're done he'll help us set a wrong aright.

Ryk. Unless ye be some realm-traversing devils, (good Luck with that on many levels. Hee-hee-hee-heeee.)

Dro. As I'm a man the wyrm will understand our plight, and he will fight beside us once our tale is told.

Ryk. I'm sure you'd make a manly snack; if minds a dragon not a little mold. I fear however you will find him disincline'd to make a feast on words nor fowl nor man nor beast.

Quik A dragon wouldn't eat a person anyway, you're thinking of the eastern sand drakes.

Ryk. Perhaps, (although I know that they can turn men into pancakes.

Mel. This minstrel is a fool, we must be on our way.

Ryk. But stay, the hour's growing late, and darkness does approach in its eternal cycle for to smother this fair day. So many dangers do lie hidden on the mountain, in the shadows where one cannot see. It would be best for thee if thou'd agree to share a camp with me. I'll sing for thee my dear, and fill thy lov'ly ear with tasty morsels of my tongue, for sweetest be the music that we make when we are young.

Quik You'll sing soprano soon if you refuse to leave her be, a parakeet can keep a tune as well as any leering cassowary.

Ryk. So young and such a wit. The trouble with a sharpen'd tongue, my little one, is you may cut yourself with it.

Dro. The girl speaks true mainlander, a lesson looms if you don't swiftly change your manner. It's best that you are gone, before the setting of the sun obscures the path that you were on.

Ryk. The fire dwindles but is not out yet. A pity, we'd have made a wonderful duet. Perhaps we'll meet again, in circumstances where we might call one another friend.

Dro. I do not think that it would be a meeting you would like.

Ryk. Ah well, it's not a nasty evening for a nature hike. My lady.

> [*Exit Rykel, whistling his earlier tune.*]

Mel. Soprano?

Quik But he-

Mel. When I have of need of my much younger sibling to protect me, I'll gladly let thee know.

Quik But I'm almost fifteen!

Mel. You just turn'd fourteen by your own admission.

Quik One ages swiftly when they're on a secret mission.

Mel. It was a secret until you-

Dro. Enough you two, the matter it is done. Some fire food and rest would now be best for ev'ryone.

Mel. I'll gather wood, you put that sling of yours to use
before it grows too late, and find us something else to eat
but moldy cheese and salted mack'rel bait.
                    [*Exeunt manet Drond.*]

Dro. Mark well your trail so that you don't get lost!
(I could not bear to lose them too, although
Already I have paid the greatest cost.
A minstrel and a fool has found me old,
And did not cower as he once would have.
An old man, old man, but of course I am.
For even fools can over wisdom trip,
When wayward foot finds some protruding tip.
Yet lacking strength I carried in my youth,
Let vengeance forge a vast reserve within,
My new blade knowledge, and my armor truth,
And bloody end this as it did begin.
Oh Thoughts who watch us from beyond the veil,
And wait to welcome give unto their harbor,
Upon the promise of thy shores I swear,)
[*Removes a locket he keeps around his neck at all times.*]
I shall avenge thee, my beloved daughter.
(As from the Orb of Unity they broke,
Creating time itself that we might love,
So shall I break from reason for revenge,
In memory of she they robb'd me of.
What father would not forgo all restraint
To see the man who stole their only joy,
Who mindless murders at their master's will,
Deliver'd to the darkness of the void.
Though well protected be this butcherer,
A dragon does not shy from any shield,
So I shall say to *Monwyrm* what I must,
To bait his unrestrain'd bloodthirstiness,
If countless be the deaths his ire yield.

Keratin claws to clash with strongest steel,
Serrated teeth to tear through armor'd flesh,
And if his mission any more require,
Let all the world be burn'd in dragon fire.)
Be man who took you monster born or made,
No peace I'll find until he lifeless lay.
This I do swear. [Kisses locket and replaces it.]

[*Exeunt.*]

Act I, Scene 2

[The head and Torso of Sir Ekinroy Carthagian of North Kalas emerge from beneath massive ribs. A black mask surrounds his eyes.]

Ekin. (Ah. It would appear that thou hast come upon me in a state of some distress. Fear not, my manservant *Rykel* has gone to fetch assistance, for I know he would do nothing less. I see that some of you have flagons on your person. *Rykel* most recently retain'd mine own. Hydration is essential, that is certain. I must admit I could have us'd a drop ere he had gone. I'll not make light nor lie, upon my bladder lies a weighty matter, but better I would say to keep important reaches wet than breeches dry. Persistent pressure can become a crushing burden to the consciousness as well. Fight as I might, mine eyes attempt to seek the realm where dreams do dwell. A knight need not comply however, to compression that might cause another man to tire. If anyone should come across my, squirrely little squire…) *[Closes eyes.]*
Dro. Watch where you step; and watch your head.
Quik You can't watch both. Can you smell that?
Mel. I think something is dead.

[Enter Melsyne, Drond, Quik.]
Quik I've heard it's dark and dank where dragon's dwell, but nothing could prepare you for the smell.

[Ekinroy lets out a long, loud yawn. The travelers go to their knees.]

Dro. Oh mighty master, prince among your peers, please lend your ears to these humble Natirans who have travell'd far to find thee here. A tragic tale to tell has turn'd us hither, hoping beyond bounds of hope to gain your grace, and sue for justice only thee might swift deliver, much relying on the magnanimity of thy immortal race. A bargain we would beg if be so bold, a favor gain a favor fairly give, as did our ancestors in days of old. Revenge we seek upon an evil and a fearsome foe, and would repay thy aid with aught thou could request, though be it nothing less than blood and bone. What say thee stately one?

Ekin. Thy words, Natiran-oooh, fall not on ears of stone.

Dro. Long known as noble has thy nature been, accompani'd by all thy stori'd deeds, thou wilt find naught but awe from us dear friend, for know our people still do worship thee.

Ekin. 'Tis true my exploits are quite famous, and my courage is unmatch'd, a bargain I will strike with thee; with certain-aaah, strings attach'd.

Dro. Of course–of course, oh most courageous one, but name thy price and thrice consider thy majestic will be done.

Ekin. Have I thy word thy cause is both a worthy and an, upright one?

Dro. We would not waste thy precious time with less than retribution for the heinousest of crimes. The wantonness of will was shown by he who in our blackest thoughts do keep, would cause the jealous thoughts within their darkne'd star to weep.

Ekin. Then swear do I upon my very life to set the matter right, but first, thou must help, extricate this noble knight-uuuh.

Dro. A noble knight your greatness? We do not understand.

Ekin. Thou clearly came to find Sir *Ekinroy Carthagian*, and so if thou wouldst be so kind to quickly lend a helping-aaah, hand?

Dro. What have you done you fool? this cannot be.

Ekin. My duty have I done good sir, and slain this vicious beast for king and country.

Quik (At least we know what died.)

Dro. O're land and sea have journey'd we to seek this ancient creature. Through squalls and rain, traversing rough terrain, our desperation such that we would brave the brutalist barrage of nature, only to discover you, who heartless slew our long-sought savior. To kill you quickly would be kindest mercy so I'll not, instead we shall for *Monwyrm's* sake abandon you that you may slowly rot. [*Starts to leave.*]

Mel. Grandfather stop. We all have heard that dragons can be, difficult to deal with by the denizens in their immediate vicinity.

Dro. This outrage does defy all decency.

Mel. Yet how can we in all good conscience leave someone in need?

Dro. A murderer!

Mel. A man.

Dro. He lost that title when his quest for *Monwyrm's* death began. Now come, for my decision has been made.

Mel. Thy solitary will is not the final resolution in this cave. If two of three decide he should be free, then by a fair majority his life we'll duly save. My sister, wouldst thou leave this man to perish for his deed?

Quik It seems he might be more of use to us if he were freed. He did just do the most impressive thing I've ever seen. If he can best a dragon, maybe he can beat *Bazeen*.
Mel. We could not ask this thing-
Dro. How right you are granddaughter. (To leave the knight to die alone would be like sending some prize bull to slaughter.) My name is *Drond*, Sir...?
Ekin. Sir *Ekinroy* of, of, of *North Kalas*.
Dro. The lasses are my grandchildren, *Melsyne* and *Quik*.
Ekin. Well met good folk, and timely.
Mel. Well met sir knight.
Dro. We come from far *Natiro* on a confidential quest, and seek assistance setting an egregious grievance to its rest.
Ekin. Upon the souls of all my kin whose inner light-oooh, has yet to find eclipse, a secret told in confidence will ne'r escape my lips.
Dro. We sorely seek the death of a dishonorable man, who wrong'd my fam'ly such that only such a villain can. If thou wouldst rightly keep the bargain we'd have made with *Monwyrn*, were he not, deceas'd, perhaps we'll find it in our hearts to see that from thy certain doom thou art releas'd.
Mel. Be warn'd, sir knight, the quarry that we seek-
Ekin. It matters not what manner of a man he be. I am accounted by the people of my nation as the greatest of all warriors in a generation. If he be by but mortal means defended, then by my blade his life will swift be ended.
Quik (It seems humility does not affect the people of this region.)
Mel. He is protected by-
Ekin. No foe is safe from me though hide they fast behind the iron legion-oooh. But while my reputation grants me passage beyond any border, yet must I adhere

unto the sacred customs of my order. The punishment for taking life in non-defense is strict, as laid out fully in our kingdom's lawful edict; a knight may slay nor man nor beast unless that life be judg'd unworthy by at least a single lawful leader or an honorable person, in which case said knight may stand for them as rightful champion-aaah. Fair mistress, for thy saint's compulsion to stay firm against thy grandfather's desire to desert a knight in need, I judge thee fill'd of kindness fortitude and mercy-eeee, the building blocks of honor, if ever, there were any. If thou dost think this, miscreant, unfit to breath, and care not that his heirs have cause to grieve, then I shall challenge him with certainty, in thy name and that of thy family-mmmm.

Mel. This man most certain does deserve to die, but-

Ekin. Then quite content am I-I-I-I!

Quik Art thou in pain? sir knight.

Ekin. My mind has mast'ry over, pain, and all the like, but I do worry of my swiftly dimming eyesight. Art thou good people truly here in flesh, or hast thou come to welcome me unto my final rest?

Quik He'll be no use to anyone if we don't yank him from beneath this carcass soon.

Ekin. Thy eyes, fair maid, at first possess'd the light of stars, but now more that of moons.

Mel. Myself and *Quik* shall each grab hold a limb, if thou would'st help then try to lift the creature's bulbous belly as we pull on him.

Dro. Forgive us for our need, oh dear departed dragon.

Ekin. Have any of thee spirits chanc'd upon a ghostly flagon? Though earthly or ethereal the liquid lies within, I'd grant thee any favor for a drop, or ten.

Mel. One, two, three!

Ekin. Ahhhh! Thou art corporeal indeed.

Mel. Again. One, two, three!

Ekin. Ahhhhahaha! I happier was when I thought thee apparitions.
Mel. One, two, three!

[*Ekinroy is pulled free.*]

Ekin. Ahhh.
Quik. Yuck, just our luck to find our unstuck savior needs a bath.
Mel. I spied a cleansing pool lies nearby on our path.
Dro. So long as sharp his sword remains, reflexes quick and muscles thick, our pains may not have been for naught. (Regardless of the smell we may have well uncover'd such a sacrificial savior as the lost have often sought.) What right have we? to fight the fickleness of fate, perhaps indeed we have not come too late.
Ekin. [*Lying on his back.*] I'll ne'r take breathing air again for granted, for even in this hot sulfuric den I find my life-preserving wind enchanted. The beastly burden being lifted from my chest, my senses do recall the reminiscence of a quest.
Dro. Oh yes, a bargain there was fairly made between us; if your mem'ry does not fail by some convenience.
Ekin. My memory is such that mortal men may envy, and true I do remember I did enter in the service of the lady.
Dro The service of us all.
Ekin. To claim a challenge in thy family's name I do recall, yet sworn upon the honor of the lady, whose fiats I shall follow till I triumph or I fall. Assuming thou art in agreement all, no conflict should be caus'd by a discrepancy so small.
Dro. Hmph.
Ekin. Oh do not grumble now my newfound friend, for thou shalt see how humbl-y a knight of *North Kalas* does

keep his word. Young lass if I may ask a favor once again, wouldst thou be kind enough as to procure my sword?

Mel. Go on, his struggle surely must have been exhausting, and for what he swore to help us with it's only fair.

Quik Exhausting? Who knows how long the lazy sot's been lying there?

Mel. Quik…

Ekin. It's true I too long underneath the dragon lay.

Quik Ahhhh, it's cover'd in some nasty grimy paste.

Ekin. I sorely long for freshness in the air and light of day.

Quik Here.

Ekin. I thank thee little one, now if thou wouldst be kind enough to help support me just above the waste?

Quik What?

Ekin. My leg is broken, I must use thee as a crutch until the bone might be set back in place.

Quik Oh great.

Dro. I tried to tell thee he could not be trusted, making bargains knowing well his leg already had been busted.

Ekin. I was not certain 'til I tried to stand, yet still it is a simple fix my cranky comrade; I have a plan. I know a man, a mender and a friend, blessed by the Thoughts with an ability internally to mend.

Dro. A witch doctor?

Ekin. His magic is a marvel to behold, a mender strong as any in the stories told of old. A fortnight only for to find us where he does abide, or three days ride, for he within the kingdom of fair *Crysin* does reside.

Quik The land of magic?

Ekin. It is a kingdom much like most, more tolerant of mystic powers though I do suppose. But first of course our course must take us to *Garban*.

Dro. Each moment that we squander on your sad incompetence delays the profess'd promise of our recompense.

Ekin. But surely thou wilt want to be rewarded by my king, for saving his most decorated knight is no small thing. Such stories bards shall tell and songs they'll sing of thy fair deed, thy names shall be immortaliz'd as those who saw the knight was freed. And too our clergy must remove the curse they plac'd upon me ere I left.

Mel. Thou hast been curs'd?

Ekin. More like a boon bestowed at my own behest, by ancient custom to be sent into a temporary banishment. A promise to my people not to waiver, 'til the dragon was destroy'd and so complete my labor. This mask of ebon on my face is such that only sacred ceremony can erase. And until then, I am invisible to all my countrymen.

Quik Invisible? As in, invisible?

Ekin. Essentially, acknowledgment of one who wears the mask of willing death is strictest breaching of propriety.

Quik (Well that's not silly.)

Dro. At least the dragon might have help'd or harm'd us instantly, much better than a drawn out death by sheer stupidity.

Mel. Well I for one would welcome the diversion, I have seen little of the world beyond our island and my military service. We are completely out of leads, what if this king has knowledge of our quarry or his deeds? It is no long delay, we hardly have a host of choices anyway, and so I see no reason not to gain the knowledge of some unseen sights along the way.

Ekin. Art thou a soldier lady?

Mel. A six-year vet'ran of the battles at the Split I am. Dost thou dare care to comment from perspective of a North Kalasian man?

Ekin. I too have travell'd south to face the hellish turmoil of that place, and fought along with female hosts from *Myradawn*, as well as other nation's women I accounted brave and strong. But my years in Alnorda's never ending war do number only three.
Mel. I'm likely somewhat older than art thee.
Quik She's twenty five.
Mel. Quik…
Dro, Well I have seen it twenty seven times.
Ekin. Good sir, forgive me for I never could have known. Art thou that legendary *Drond* made famous for the constant valor though hast shown? That *Drond* whose oaken staff and shining steel so oft has caus'd the enemy to yield?
Mel. That was some time ago. He does not like to speak of it in unfamiliar company.
Ekin. Forgive me lady.
Mel. *Melsyne*, since we may long be travelling together.
Ekin. Then call me Ekinroy.
Quik And call me *Quik*, cause, that's my name; (and because I'm clever.)
Dro. We did not rescue him to make a friend. Attachment to a man condem'd to fight our enemy may poorly end. Unless we plan to spend our lives inside a rotting dragon's tomb, I strongly do suggest we start this doomed quest for magic that can somehow mend a wound.
Mel. Yes, off let's be to see the famed golden dome of thy *Garban*, then leave thy homeland for more places I had only dreamt to someday see and understand.
Quik An easy thing to sue for sights to see while nothing leans on thee to make thee tire.
Ekin. It's only till we find my faithful squire, young *Quik*.
Quik Just *Quik*.

Dro. *Rykel* can well relieve thee presently, his sacred duty is supporting me. A burden he will gladly bear I'm sure, so giddy will he be to see his master's safe return.
Quik I thought no one could look at you.
Ekin. Exceptions clearly must be made for servants in one's retinue.
Quik We came to seek a dragon and we find a stinky stuck-up knight instead. A cursed and a crippl'd knight no less, who clearly hit his head. (Invisible indeed. I am too young to be a crutch.)
Ekin. I must admit I was surpris'd to find *Rykel* not waiting for me when I fell'd my foe. I hope no harm did come to him as I did battle *Monwyrm* on the mountain slope. Alas, he likely ran for aid not wholly knowing where upon me *Monwyrm* lay. I hope to pick his trail up as we travel hence, and so unravel the true reason for his absence.
Dro. Just don't forget you owe a debt we will not be forgiving, 'til you grant the service that old *Monwyrm* might have, were he living.
Ekin. Of course, oh ancient and heroic one; just one more simple but essential thing,
Dro. Now what?
Ekin. A trinket I must bring unto my king. Presenting him old *Monwyrm's* tooth is necessary proof of his demise, and too the tooth must be us'd in the ritual to bring this dead knight back to life.
Quik (Metaphoric'lly.)
Ekin. All dragons do possess one special fang that stories say maintains the essence of the creature. Let us retrieve it swiftly and be on our way, before it's stumbl'd on by some dishonorable treasure seeker. Please help me *Quik* unto the dragon's maw.
Quik (The Prince of Dragons surely wasn't light, but I would say the same about a single-legged knight.)

Ekin. I should prepare thee all for *Rykel's* surly manner I
suppose, for some have said he does not show the
necessary def'rence of a squire, yet I believe the roughest
of exteriors oft hides the kindest heart a chest can sire.
[Exeunt.]

Wouldst thou be kind enough to lend thy dagger friend?
My thanks. Now let us fish within.
Quik That's nasty.
Ekin. Though on occasion we conflict on what is wrong
and what is right, I feel I have well train'd *Rykel*, and do
believe that someday he may make an honorable…
Thief!

Act I, Scene 3

[Enter hooded Wizard, whose face is never revealed.]
Enter Bazeen, who kneels.]

Wiz. *Bazeen.*
Baz. Your humble servant Greatest One.
Wiz. Should I assume since you are here the deed is done?
Baz. The pair rest soundly in their native soil.
Wiz. It was your clumsiness that did create this turmoil.
Baz. Yes, ancient lord. *[Rises.]* Though none could have foreseen a chance encounter with a fishing boat, the ordain'd meeting place was quite remote.

[The Wizard clenches his fist and Bazeen is slammed back down to his knees.]

Wiz. None, my champion?
So many mighty assets I command,
And you with access to them all, my hand.
Such men and gold and horses, massive ships,
Mariners and mercenaries many,
All sworn to mass on orders from your lips
And stand against the strongest enemy.
More battle-tested warriors quick to cluster,
That kings could scarcely hope so much to muster.
Enough to spread a net and catch a fleet
Of any boats so bold to brave the sea;
And yet one dingy dinghy does decide
To side up to my trusted champion,

Whose mission was in secrecy to send
A missive to our terrible new friend,
Who naught on this side of the cursed Split
Could help but hinder, harm, and swift condemn,
Who none may know of our newfound accord
For it would much endanger us and them,
And you allow this bantam flotsam skiff
To stumble on in your insanity,
A meeting may decide the final fate
Of all the people of Alnorda; nay,
Indeed the fate of all humanity?
Baz. [*Stands.*] I don't believe they knew what they so
boldly stumbl'd-

[*The Wizard gestures and Bazeen is knocked roughly to
the ground. Bazeen climbs back to his knees.*]

Wiz. And then when they had seen what they should not,
The dingy dinghy drifts away again,
And disappears before your multitude
Of minions care to see that it is caught.
A military man, a strategist,
A mercenary fear'd even afore
He sought within my service to enlist;
Do tell me, in your vast experience,
Did any tutor teach you how to set
A man'd perimeter as a defense?
Baz. Of course, Great One. A strong perimeter was set.
The boat, however, was so small that not a single trusted
scout did see it.
Wiz. They did not see it for it was so small.
Baz. Natiran fishing boats are barely large enough to
boast a crew of two or three, and rarely are they found so
far out in the open sea.
Wiz. These, interlopers on their fishing boat,

Who drifted far enough from shore to float
Where boats their size are rarely found at all,
Do you believe they manag'd to bring in
A healthy haul?
Baz. Great One?
Wiz. Do you think that they caught a lot of fish?
Baz. I wish I knew most nobl-est of lords.
Wiz. Was that not what they came there to accomplish?
Baz. I had assume'd so.
Wiz. Then I'll assume that you have studi'd not
The migratory patterns of what's caught
Among the southern shoals I chose to be
Our carefully selected meeting spot.
A place I pick'd precisely for I knew,
Natirans would not fish for fish were few.
Baz. Most wise, your wizardness. An angle that I wish I
had explor'd-
Wiz. This means of course they were not there for sport,
Or for to feed their hungry families,
But rather to discover and report,
Which makes them our most cunning enemies.
It's clear that some opposing element
Caught wind that emissaries would be sent
And some important meeting would ensue,
So sent they spies to seek our rendezvous.
One of my brothers if I were to guess,
An irksome thorn I someday must address.
But how did wind of what was to transpire,
Find fertile ears in someone else's hire?
Baz. Oh great one, I would never dare betray you.
Wiz. Our magic bond ensures that you speak true.
Yet members of your, ruthless retinue,
Might not know loyalty so well as you.
And too they might not fear me as they should,
Their closeness to you makes them feel protected.

Baz. There were a handful of my faithful men, with whom I did our course confide within, but told only the best in my employ we ready made to meet a secret envoy.

[*The Wizard raises his hand and four mercenaries fall dead from the wings.*]

Wiz. Perhaps next time you'll make a point to find
More quiet men whom thou dost in confide.
You fill your ranks with cut-throats rogues and thieves,
Pray this time you find better men than these.
Baz. I shall replace them with the best thy coin can buy.
Wiz. Complacency corrupts the weak mankind,
And so this threat create I by design.
To strengthen their resolve is all I seek,
In doing, one must sometimes cull the weak.
The Father grows complacent in his tower,
While weakness spreads its wings like a disease,
Afear'd to wield his thought begotten power,
Where I would ply that power as I please.
The war our efforts beg to bring about
Does but begin a blessed turnabout,
For nothing less would I betray a brother,
Than someday to become the blessed father.
Peace and harmony are fine to strive for,
But nothing changes fortunes like a war.
Baz. [*Rising to his feet.*] Your war will happen, this I swear, for both are dead who hop'd to interfere.
Wiz. Tell truthful what befell them, and in full,
No usual half-hearted doggerel.
It was a deed discreetly done I trust?
Baz. Twas but a woman and a man who must have ran soon as their feet did hit the land. Their haste alerted loyal shorebound men, who rode them down and apprehended them. When I arriv'd they had the couple

bound, awaiting at their farm far from the nearest town. The pair had kill'd three of my company, so I saw fit to see that they died slowly.

Wiz. There were no others at this, country farm?

Baz. Not who did know enough to cause us harm. An aged fellow and two younger folk did pass as from the farm we rode. We heard their screams when they did reach the scene, but bodies always will be found eventually.

Wiz. These likely friends or fam'ly of our spies,
Between them who do boast three pairs of eyes,
Did pass they close enough to see your face?

Baz. But briefly for we set a steady pace.

*[The wizard gestures and Bazeen is thrown to the ground
again. Bazeen rises back to his feet.]*

A boy, a girl, and one old man are hardly any threat to thy well though-out plan. My agents were not bashful with their knives, it's likely they are hiding for their lives.

Wiz. Three pairs of eyes attach to triple mouths.

Baz. Three mouths afraid to let their secrets out.

Wiz. No death goes uninvestigated true?
Investigating might lead back to you,
and many know of our affiliation,
Your face comes with a famed reputation.
So find these folk and finish what's begun,
You won't be welcome here until it's done.

Baz. It may prove challenging to find them lord-

*[Bazeen flies backward, sliding awkwardly to a stop.
Bazeen rises to his feet.]*

I left my armor on my horse Great one. When next we meet, remind me I should leave it on.

Wiz. Go finish what you started at the farm, *Bazeen*.
Baz. They breathe their final breaths as we do speak.
[*Bazeen bows, turns to leave.*]
Wiz. *Bazeen*. I'll not abide the next loose end. Your life
is coin I'm quite willing to spend.

[*Exeunt.*]

Act I, Scene 4
[Enter Bandit #1, Bandit #2.]

Ban 1. [*Rolls three dice.*] A wizard and a champion. The wizard spies from out his servant's eyes; I keep two.
Ban 2. A lovely surprise. [*Rolls three.*] The king's army, bitter brew, I can keep three but only half the total counts for me.
Ban 1. I challenge you.
Ban 2. I will accept, if I get half an ally when I choose.
Ban 1. Agreed; your lucky die though stays with me.
Ban 2. It's fair enough to have a try, but only if the ally wins a tie.

[Bandit #1 grunts affirmative.]

The challenger rolls first.

[Bandit #1 rolls two dice.]

[Enter Bandit #3 at a run.]
Ban 3. Our fortune changes for the better.
Ban 2. Your timing is the worst. I must be one with these fair bones. [*Rolls three dice. Loses.*] Oh curse the cow they came from and the carver's fam'ly home.
Ban 1. One round to me, one more makes mine the best two out of three.
Ban 3. Well hurry up and have it done, four trav'llers come.
Ban 1. Shhh. How can an honest bandit concentrate.

Ban 3. Our banditry may want if we do wait; what have you got?
Ban 2. A wizard and his champion; may he rot.
Ban 3. And you?
Ban 2. The army of the king; but win a tie and have a half an ally.

[They roll again in succession. Bandit 2 wins.]

That's one apiece.
Ban 1. Oh damn your dirty luck, I aim to end your streak.
Ban 2. Too bad you suck, your outlook does look bleak.
Ban 3. Some strangers do approach we may waylay.
Ban 1. The king himself could come but we must play.

[They roll in succession.]

Ban 2. The outcome hinges on my ally.
Ban 3. Your half an ally.

[Bandit #2 rolls a lone die. Loses.]

Bandits Ahhh!
Ban 2. Some regiment of dwarves come from the North? Lame.
Ban 1. But half an ally did you call and half an ally came.
Ban 2. What will you take for winnings lucky skunk?
Ban 1. The wine sack which you pilfer'd from that monk.
Ban 2. Well that suits me just fine.
Ban 1. Why's that?
Ban 2. I finish'd all the wine.

Ban 3. If you two outlaws would your weapons out, we have an ambush we must be about. For four unlucky trav'lers casu'l come, an old man and a cripple and two female ones.

Ban 1. It sounds to me too good for to be true.

Ban 2. Most likely but what have we else to do? I'm out of stolen trinkets; so are you.

Ban 3. Let hide us then and apprehend new hostages and inventory.

[*The bandits hide.*]

[*Enter Melsyne, Drond, Ekinroy supported by Quik.*]

Ekin. Eyes close and somewhat beady? An odd twitch to his lengthy nose?

Mel. Dishevel'd hair, a nervous manner, ragged clothes?

Ekin. In bearing over-proud, his speech a nasal sound, a smile that comes easily?

Mel. We speak of the exact same man, in affectation, rather weaselly.

Ekin. And how big was the bag he carri'd with him?

Mel. A size I'd wager one could fit a dragon's tooth within.

Ekin. The signs were there but my hope made me blind, for most ill-gotten gain, *Rykel* left me behind.

Mel. How is it *Ekinroy*, that such a scandalous companion came into thy company?

Ekin. His mother, rest her sole, was in the employ of my family. A saintly woman of whom no fault could be found. Upon her deathbed begg'd she that I do my best to turn his wayward ways around. And so took I the rascal as my squire, hoping to install some virtue in him, sadly virtue never grew he to admire, the maturation of his manner slim. Unfounded was her total trust in me, and

though I strove to honor her fair memory, I fear I fail'd
my childhood maid completely.
Mel. It sounds as thou didst all that thy could, a bad seed
will not grow though soil be good. Thou offer'd sunlight
yet he chose the shade; her memr'y well is honor'd with
the efforts thou hast made.
Ekin. I've not heard kinder words most gentle lady,
thank thee truly for thy insight and thy courtesy.

[*Melsyne whips a dagger from her boot to clean her
nails.*]

Thy wisdom's only equal'd by the quality of thy
concealed weaponry.
Mel. Natiran warriors have their weapons forg'd
befitting personality. The phoenix on the hilt was built
with my unique skillset in mind, for while I sometimes
stumble when surrounded with an overwhelming
strength, I always keep my wits and even stronger will I
rise.
Ekin. Thy metal is most pleasing to mine eyes.
Quik If you continue staring at my sister's arsenal, and
find her finely forged metal fine, I'll gladly place my
dagger to your jugular and see how outward pleasing you
find mine.
Ekin. I nothing meant suggestive by my comment. My
sweet betrothed waits for me at home, fair *Gwendolyn*
with hair as golden as, the sunset.
Quik (The sunsets I have seen were pink.)
Ekin. Thou'lt meet her soon, and she may well inspire
thee to song.
Quik (I highly doubt that so I think.)
Mel. She is so beautiful?
Ekin. Such earthly concepts do her mighty wrong, mere
beauty is a cart that she a comely horse but pulls along.

And virtuous, a falling star that blinds a lover by its light,
a fallen angel burning in the sky at night. She is a sponge
that does absorb the darkness of a tainted soul, and too
the squirrel what tucks a winters worth of sustenance
within its hidden hole. So see my dear young newly-
founded friend, I've not a single bone that would be led
astray to some unplumed end.
Quik Then how art thou off fighting dragons on a lonely
mountain, whilst she sits as safely as the lowest coin
within a sacred fountain?
Ekin. Without mine honor I am not the man she loves.
Indeed it was my *Gwendolyn*, spurr'd by the Thoughts
above, who did convince me that the time was nigh, to
slay the beast and not return until I triumph or I die.
Quik (Oh is that so?)
Ekin. With much insistence did she bid me go; 'Ride
forth and sacrifice thyself my love, for thy death shall
much please the Thoughts above', she did proclaim.
'Confront the dragon in his awful cave, and offer up thy
simple earthly life, for freedom only comes when thou art
brave, and we shall only flourish from thy strife. As
thirsty soil is saturated by thy blood, so spreads the
nourishment that speeds the growth of our
unconsummated love.'
Ban 1. [*Reveals themself.*] You'll speed the growth of
daisies should I have my way, for never such a simp'ring
twat have I waylaid.
Dro. Who are you stranger? to harass us honest travelers,
with naked steel held in a nervous hand?

[*Bandits #2 and #3 reveal themselves.*]

Ban 2. Who are we three you mean old man.
Dro. Old man again? I grow so weary of this land.

[*They fight. Drond and Melsyne each slay a bandit. Exit Bandit #3. Quik drops Ekinroy, then mimes throwing a dagger and we hear a grunt of pain offstage.*]

Ekin. [*Readjusting to his human crutch.*] These men were soldiers once, considering their gear.
Mel. How could thy kingdom tolerate deserters such as these did hap upon us here? What circumstance would make a North Kalasian soldier turn to banditry?
Ekin. Hard times *Melsyne*. The finest soldier will despair when wages will not feed their family.
Dro. What rubbish. Times always will seem hard to men whose wills are weak. Natirans all have work enough to keep us honest, children learn to fish and cook and keep a weapon keen. From early age our chores are heap'd upon us, that we'll never want for lack of monetary means. We are to occupi'd to render cries for compensation we deem insufficient in its size.
Ekin. Did I describe fair *Gwendolyn's* hypnotic eyes? As blue as is the clearest stream they are.
Quik (Please no more convoluted metaphors.)
Dro. I hope this king of yours is not too far. More bandits may be hiding in the pines, we'll pile these as warnings for more soldier's who've succumb'd to, hard times.

[*Exit Drond and Melsyne, each dragging a bandit off.*]

Ekin. And features so supremely delicate, they scarcely can support their modest weight.
Quik I have no sympathy; supporting yours is far the worser fate.

[*Exeunt.*]

Act II, Scene 1

[Enter Crier, blowing a trumpet poorly and seemingly at random.]

Cri. (What's all the ruckus crier? Has vicious *Monwyrn* come to finish off our kingly sire? Of course not captive comrades in thy cushy thrones, dids't thou not hear delight within my dulcet tones? Such joyous notes can mean one single thing alone; the dragon's dead and *Ekinroy* is home!) *[Blows trumpet.]*

[Enter Citizen #1.]
Cit 1. The dragon it is dead you say?
Cri. Indeed, from under wing of bleak reptilian tyranny, our kingdom has been freed.
Cit 1. Then play the happiest of melodies. *[Blows trumpet.]*

[Enter Citizen #2.]
Cit 2. Did I hear right? The dragon-
Cri/Cit 1. Dead.
Cit 2. By Thoughts we are delivered; how fares the knight?
Cri. (So bloodi'd one might barely know it's him,
And burn'd from crown to now misshapen foot,
A vacant hole where once there liv'd a limb,
His hair all sing'd, replac'd by cak'd on soot.
Physicians sure will ply their healing arts,
So they may say they did all that they could,
But any pray'rs reside within thy hearts,

Then say them while they may still do some good.
His haunted and exhausted countenance,
Unseeing eyes and heavy si-olence,
His pleas to mercif'lly be dispatch'd hence,
Bespeak a man succumb'd to violence.)
Cit 2. He sav'd us all but won't survive the fight.
Cri. I've heard it said he might not last the night.
Cit 2. (Behold the bold Sir *Ekinroy* has sacrific'd himself
to save our kingdom!)
[*Exit Citizen #2.*]

Cit 1. To witness such a grizzly sight as our heroic
mangl'd knight must be a heavy burden on the young. I
thank thee for the courage it must take to oft relive such
vile visions by the service of thy tongue.
Cri. Oh I've not seen the man myself I must admit; to be
the first to bring such news one must embellish, just a bit.
Cit 1. Relating rumor as reality is morally corrupt. If
you've no trusted source to sight, aren't you in essence
just making it up?
Cri. A crier must create the truth by telling people what
they care to hear. I'm not the worst I fear, for tis the
fashion to appear perceptive as you shout from off a
bias'd box. (My main competitor is one so sly they call
him, Fox.) [*Blows trumpet.*]
Cit 1. Beware the criers claiming they are wise, they
cover verbal canvases with lies!
[*Exeunt.*]

[*Enter Melsyne, Drond, Ekinroy, Quik.*]
Ekin. Behold good people our fair city of Garban.
Dro. This brand of fair translates to filthy in our land. By
beauty I'll assume you mean deformity, for
wholesomeness I will insert depravity; a warren of
forlorn and falling hovels, contrasted here and there by

gaudy opulence, a complex tapestry of all that could be cobbl'd, overflowing with a pack'd-in populace.

Mel. Is that the famed golden dome off in the distance?

Quik It's even bigger than the tales do tell.

Ekin. Thou wilt be welcome there for thy assistance, and I shall show thee all the places I know well. Beneath resides the court of our good king, his palace all that one might dare to dream.

Dro. (By dream I do assume he means a nightmare.)

Ekin. However ere we sojourn there, sweet sustenance, some honest council and a much-requir'd cleansing do await at this estate, for *Cragmyre* does become more vex'd by guests who are untidy than by those arriving late.

Dro. Refresh yourself and gossip if you must, *Melsyne* and I are well content to wait.

Ekin. The hospitality that lies within should not be disregarded so, dost thou not wish to wash the dust off from the road?

Dro. Such frippery is not for me and mine, who care less for appearance than for information we might find.

Mel. Is this thy fam'ly home Sir *Ekinroy*?

Ekin. Nay, 'tis that of Sir *Gyle*, a brother since I was a boy. A better and benevolenter friend was never found, so trustworthy to end the need to ever have a loyal hound. Indeed such faith had I in he I did entrust him with the safety of my lady as I was unto the vi-le wyrm's lair bound. I knew of none you see who'd keep so close a watch as he, for he had something of a friendship with her before me. Some brief encounter when she toil'd in the entertainment industry; though details seem to 'scape their memories.

[*Ekinroy approaches the door, still supported by Quik.*]

This door has ne'r before unbolted been. Oh loving lady and my loyal friend, triumphant I return to thee!
[Exit Ekinroy, Quik.]

Mel. An elder much respected said to me the gravest insult was declining hospitality. A soldier who so claim'd the insult to the other was unto thyself the same, for soldiers, he did say, could rarely know from whence the next meal came

Dro. Thy elder has grown wiser since, and should not be subjected to such insolence.

Mel. Then let me speak it plainly to thy face; thy animosity is out of place. This sacrificial lamb we've sav'd has no idea the nature of his prey. It is a wizard's champion whose death we seek, not some misguided farmer lost his way. Whomever takes his life will die within the week, as promis'd by the brotherhood from olden days.

Dro. A better death than rotting in a cave. I will not dine with our young dragon slayer, nor clean up to meet a foreign king. A word might turn this monarch to our jailer, having done and on our way's the wisest thing. 'Twould not be good to grow attach'd to him, and all these strange unnatural mainland ways.

Mel. Between deceptive and unnatural, more honest is it to be strange.

Ekin. Good *Gwendolyn* didst I just hear thee moan? Who does inside assail my fair betroth'd? But force the bedroom door young *Quik*, my leg is still too weak to splinter wood so thick.

Quik Gladly!

[Sound of the door being kicked repeatedly.]

Ekin. Fear not my love thy fearless knight has come, and shall evacuate whoe'r does violate thy sanctum!
Mel. Should we not help him?

[*Trumpet.*]

[*Enter Crier, King Cragmyre, Royal Guard #1, Royal Guard #2.*]
Cri. All hail his royal majesty, King *Cragmyre* of North Kalas. [*Blows trumpet.*] All hail companions of Sir *Ekinroy*, ye far off foreign nobles in disguise, who may be friends; (but also may be spies.)
Crag. Well met my noble friends. I am King *Crag-*

[*Trumpet.*]

Enough young one, thy trumpet is uneasy on our royal ear. Disperse some coin that it might be repair'd.

[*Royal Guard #1 hands the crier a small coin purse.*]

Cri. (The crown itself does now support the crier, I shall tailor truth to suit the ear of my employer; Fox will eat his tail!)
                [*Exit Crier with a final trumpet blast.*]

Crag. King *Cragmyre* is my name, but, (you already knew that.)
Dro. Your Majesty, we are-
Crag. Is't true that you accompany Sir *Ekinroy*?
Dro. He travels with us, honor-bound beyond other employ.
Crag. Not beyond my employ, I am his king, no foreign ties outweigh the signet on this ring.
Dro. Your knight might still be in his prison if-

Mel. Your Majesty, we came seeking your famous wisdom.

Crag. A diplomatic tongue, for one so lovely and so young. We must have you up to the palace soon, and get those rags off you. My stylist could do wonders with that hair, oh yes, the makings of a foreign beauty are all there. Do tell to me the name does grace this pleasing face?

Mel. I am *Melsyne*, and this my grandsire *Drond*, it is a desp'rate quest that we are on.

Crag. I would hear more of thee before thou leav'st my sight, but first explain how tis thou came across my, most courageous knight.

Mel. We went to beg a bargain with the dragon, as Natirans often have of old, to offer any earthly service unto him, if he would grant us vengeance for our slaughter'd kin, whose cruelly murder'd forms are hardly cold. We came upon Sir *Ekinroy* instead, his body pinn'd beneath old *Monwyrm*, who was-

Crag. Dead?

Mel. Dead.

Crag. [*To Royal Guard #1*.] Did she say dead?

RG 1. She did.

Crag. Oh gladly will I pay up on my wagers for this happy news. [*He gives coins to both Royal Guardsmen, then flips one to an audience member*] To think I thought the man a braggart and a fool. He truly slew the awful beast, it's not some kind of foreign jest?

Mel. The dragon's carcass rots within it's nest.

Crag. Rejoice! Rejoice I say! And let the trumpets; (well, perhaps another day). We must prepare a feast, our finest vestments don.

[*Enter Gwendolyn at a run, scantily clad.*]

Gwen. Oh! Some members of the court I've come upon; (and strangers too.) You're majesty, forgive my current

state, I was, attack'd of late you see, and forc'd to flee
most prematurely.

Crag. Make no apology; forgiveness for a lady in a shift
does give the swiftest rise in me.

    [*Enter Sir Gyle in a similar state to Gwendolyn.*]

Sir *Gyle*? Thour't drench'd in sweat and look a-fright. Do
not come nearer if thou hast a fever, but explain this
awkward public sight. Decorum is expected of a-

    [*Enter Ekinroy, Quik.*]

Ekin. Deceiver, villain, vagabond and rogue,
Unholy offspring of a demon and a, gnome.
I challenge thee most foul monstrosity;
Turn not thy face from my ferocity.

Crag. What fracture now exists between my two most
faithful knights? Ye brothers friends and comrades of so
many fights?

Ekin. A chasm rent by foulest deeds my King,
A width to make the Split a paltry thing;
This creature has accosted *Gwendolyn*,
Befouling her with forced carnal sin!
With forked tongue and truth-concealing eyes,
The beast to whom I did entrust her care,
Unknowingly did coil'd wait to strike
Within its very own reptilian lair.
A vile act of unrequited lust
To spread a friendships ashes to the dust.
Fear not my loving recently betroth'd,
Thy honor need not suffer on its own,
For even in my weaken'd broken state,
I'll cut the head from off this lying snake.

Gyle Your Majesty, I beg you hear my honest plea, these
charges he doth lay on me are false!

Ekin. And even when the snake is run aground,

The truth can nowhere on its forked tongue be found.
Gyle I willingly admit that many sins I did commit, but willing was the one with whom I did commit them with; (indeed she did implore to many more commit with me.)
Ekin. (This serpent is most cunning in its lingual capacity.)
Crag. Thou art denounc'd by one who challenges with steel, it is not I to whom thou must appeal. An honest knight and true accuses thee, it is to he that thou must plead for mercy.
Gyle I cannot plead with he who challeng'd me, for when I look his way no man I see.
Ekin. No man am I now dog? No man? Thou dare?
Gyle That's not to say that were he truly here, Sir *Ekinroy* of grand *Garban* would be accounted less than any man. I cannot, could not, look on him were he at hand. Said knight was marked with the mask of death, we both were present when the magic took effect. It is, would be, against tradition were he seen by me.
Crag. I will admit, thou hast a valid argument.
Dro. (Mainlanders.)
Crag. Enough from you, who are a visitor, there is a simple way to settle such a matter. Girl.
Quik What me, Your Majesty?
Crag. Yes thee; I trust thou'rt not a simpleton?
Quik Oh no, it's only hard to speak because my unseen burden simply ways a ton.
Crag. There is an object carri'd by one close to you I do presume, which may allow normality to soon resume. Let us today allay these wretched wrongs. Present to me the tooth and for thy part in this heroic tale thou'lt be immortaliz'd in songs.
Quik The vast majority of heroes in the songs are dead; I'd rather be the simpleton thou seem to see in me and keep my head.

Crag. Impertinence, have you the monster's magic
tooth?
Ekin. The tooth was ripp'd untimely from old
Monwyrm's maw in truth. Whilst I was caught beneath
the carcass of the beast, my manservant saw fit to see to
its release.
Quik I have receiv'd upsetting news Your Majesty,
apparently, the tooth was taken by thy brave knight's
manservant whilst he himself was caught beneath the
carcass of the beast. That is what I have heard from my
unnoticeable source at least.
Crag. By all the Thoughts this does grow most
unordinary.
Dro. (Oh now it is unordinary.)
Mel. Grandfather hush, we all can do without your
commentary.
Crag. I will confess no protocol exists to fix an
unforeseen anomaly as this. The tooth must be recover'd
ere this duel proceed, and thou new friends I hope will
help perform the deed. For no assistance can be given
from within these lands. I am afraid my brave Natirans,
Sir *Ekinroy's* erection rests within thy helpful hands.

[*Royal Guard #2 whispers in Cragmyre's ear.*]

Crag. What did I say? [*Another whisper.*] Oh. His
resurrection rests within thy hands. Recover thou the
tooth we sadly lack, that with it we might bring our dead
friend back. Sir *Gyle* shall await within a cell.
Gyle But Majesty-
Crag. You've nothing more to tell. The ghost of *Ekinroy*
would never lie, for honesty has been his fault of old,
you'll answer to the man when he's alive, till then you
can appeal unto the mold. Take him away.

RG 1. Ain't your name *Roselyn*? From over at the 'Orn and Penny?

RG 2. Not likely for I know this girl, 'er name is Mistress Jenny.

Gwen. You are mistaken sirs, I came here from a nunnery.

RG 1. The beads we us'd were not a rosary.

RG 2. She ain't who you recall you twit for I knew Jenny well, she was a regular attraction at the Salty Crab Shell.

RG 1. If she told you er name was Jenny, she obviously lied, for I knew her as Roselyn; and I was satisfied.

Crag. Be quiet fools, the girl is *Ekinroy's* betroth'd; though if the hair were different, and without all the clothes; Madeline? who once attended me at Duke Bereholdt's behest?

Gwen. The same Your Majesty, I did dine at thy table this past Winterfest.

Crag. And such a Winterfest it was, what parts I can remember. No common courtesan has ever proven so enchanting; or so limber. This sheds new light on these events, this knight now needs not be confin'd so long as he repents. His punishment shall be decided at the feast, we'll make a sport of it, and at the very least Sir *Ekinroy* can say he was beguil'd by a professional.

Ekin. Can this be true once fair?

Gwen. (I aways did detest confessionals.) I sent you, I sent him off to fight a dragon. How by the Thoughts was I to know that he would saunter back again? Most men with coin want only bedding, but this one would have none of it until there was a wedding. And always with the honor and the virtue and the blah blah blah blah blah blah blah. I tried to be a lady to his lord, but I just got so bor'd.

Crag. A boring thing is chastity.

Mel. Thou art most wise oh noble king, we shall assist your recently departed knight upon his quest, the journey will be long and so a swift departure would be best.
Crag. Oh yes of course, my thanks again. And in the meantime I shall personally interrogate fair *Gwendolyn*. Off to the castle those who live and wish to play!
  [*Exeunt manet Melsyne, Drond, Ekinroy, Quik.*]

Ekin. Alas I am now thrice betray'd: by friendship, love, and even by my king.
Dro. Best not to waste thy time on pointless brooding. Assuming we are finish'd with this nonsense, might we not be on our way without a further audience?
Ekin. Of course most noble *Drond*, I now exist but to fulfill this quest that we are on. Help me away from this deceptive den of disingenuity, no longer holds my homeland any joy for me.
  [*Exeunt manet Melsyne, Drond.*]

Dro. A total waste of time as I foretold. I've never seen a poorer judge of character, a rotten minstrel servant and now this unscrupl'd fold, what harm may come from but the next egregious judgment error; I half expect this mender to be dancing on a pole.
Mel. And how are we less guilty than are they? to take advantage of a kind and trusting soul. I will not blame the hare more than the hunters place the snare; and no more noble is our goal.

  [*Exit Melsyne, Drond.*]

SUGGESTED INTERMISSION

Act II, Scene2
Enter Merchant

Mer. (What secret trinket does thy heart desire,
If thou couldst pluck it from an ancient tale?
The Maharaja's mystic sapphire,
That shows the secrets from beyond the veil?
Or maybe mad Queen Bresnahana's knot,
That traps the fae within its woven braille?
All items from all places can be got,
If through all time a mariner might sail;
The acquisition of antiquities
Is something of my humble specialty.
I'd tell thee how these items come to me;
But then I fear I could not let thee leave.
So better far to take me at my word
That most authentic is my treasur'd horde.
From juicy apple that did tempt a man
With knowledge of malevolence and good,
To journal of the one who rode the flood,
Whose knowledge Gilgamesh much coveted.
A pharos tablet from antiquity,
Restores the youth to any soul that reads,
A stylus from the air that did appear
When man politiciz'd morality.
For thee I think a very special gift,
The only in existence of its kind.
A creature I have nam'd almighty Grift;
Invisible to any but the blind.
Do tell thy friends from whence it came

But tell them to come swiftly through my door;
You see I only have three more.
                    [*Enter Rykel.*]

I also have a feather from a basilisk, a priceless nickel
made of wood, a magic trumpet that will make the
blower rich; I sold one to a crier from Garban the other
day, a means of transportation with low miles, authentic
snake oil, eternal salvation–)
Ryk. Hu-hum!
Mer. Forgive me for I did not hear thee enter. How
might a humble shopkeeper assist?
Ryk. Art thou an honest merchant?
Mer. (Of course I am.)
Ryk. Thy name is on a meager list. This city is call'd
Karborn is it not, where any item might be sold or
bought?
Mer. Why yes it is, thou art not mad, with some
exceptions any item might be had.
Ryk. (That's just my rotten luck, one honest merchant in
this vast metropolis and I stumble into the schmuck.) It
seems my senses sent me to a most unhelpful tent.
Mer. But hold my lord, by whom were you here sent?
Ryk. Why by myself you righteous proper do-good piss
ant!
Mer. You come alone, and are not in the market for an
honest merchant?
Ryk. An honest merchant would not care to see my
wares.
Mer. Secure the flap, and I'll leave off my airs. Surprise
inspections have become a problem in these modern
days, when dealing in unlawful acquisitions, much
discretion pays. I do believe I'll trust you though, you
have the look of a dishonest man.
Ryk. Such trust may be your downfall.

Mer. As long as I fall into profit if I can. A more corrupt and retched swindle-minded merchant you'll not find. You may call me Mahib, and know that long ago I left all scruples far behind. I'd gladly sell my morals if I had any, and even my own mother; if I'd not already.

Ryk. You needn't look too far to find your counterpart in crime, o' vile sir, he stands before you now, much less in common with a man than with a common cur. More stolen money have I spent on earthly pleasures than most men make fairly in a lifetime.

Mer. Respectable sir knave, but I have taken that much from the blind. I purchas'd once a poor man's hopes for but a penny, profiting enough to ransom a princess.

Ryk. A valiant feat despised gentleman, my compliments on thy success. One question; if you've seen such riches, why hast thou neglected to expand thy tent?

Mer. Alas, I've seen them come and seen them spent. I have a gambeling addiction: horses mainly, at the local track.

Ryk. Willpower is so overrated, I commend thee on thy lack. The bag about my waist contains the answer to our monetary prayers.

Mer. I beg thy pardon?

Ryk. Allow me to alleviate thy fears. [*Awkwardly unlatches the bag from his waist.*]

Mer. Ah.

Ryk. Behold once wealthy friend who shall be once again, the greatest treasure that the world has known. More valuable by far than crown or throne. Thou sayest thou hast seen resplendent riches in thy time?

Mer. More wealth than one marauder might in ten full lives of crime.

Ryk. Forgive me if all else now seems disdainful. [*Reveals the tooth.*]

Mer. That must have been quite painful.

Ryk. No moans escap'd the dragon from whose corpse it came.

Mer. A dragon's tooth you say? Why for tenpenny from a corner con I could today purchase the same. A most exquisite fake for but a novice eye or superstitious seaman's. If you give it to me, I'll hang it high above my entry; to ward away the dumber demons.

Ryk. Or find a wizard with expansive pockets, this would suck their eyeballs from their sockets.

Mer. An eyeball-sucking tooth? An abominable commodity. I'll give thee one new shiny copper for the dingy aged oddity.

Ryk. A less than tempting offer I must say, I'd take it to a wizard by myself before I so gave it away.

Mer. You do intrigue me fellow knave, I'd not have thought so little of you as to think you brave.

Ryk. A coward to the core I am, but greedy beyond measure. Within this fang you'll find a secret any mage would treasure.

Mer. You're greedy for the grave if it's a wizard that thou seek.

Ryk. They'd welcome me most cordially for this beloved trinket that I keep. No simple tooth from some pathetic wild wyrm is this, but thee one magic fang the greater monsters do possess. The tales all tell of essence that inside resides, well worthy of a kingdom for the secrets that it hides.

Mer. A magic tooth? oh my, what entertainment could this worthless talisman provide?

Ryk. Have you not heard the legend of the dragon's tooth? Wet-nurses who tell stories unto borrow'd babes have much more knowledge than do you; the captive audiences in their cribs have too.

Mer. No such dramatic fable have I heard, but your illusions I do pity. I'll take it off your hands and then direct you to a kindly gentleman resides within in the city. Give him these five unselfish coppers and he'll speak with thee for one full hour; I sent my sister to him when she thought she was a unicorn with some prophetic power. For you I do this for you are a fellow rogue; (and giving money unto those who cannot hope to pay it back is very much en vogue.)

Ryk. How kind of you, howe're the merchant just next door was well prepare'd to give his store. I would have taken it had he but own'd a little more. Perhaps I'll reconsider and become your neighbor. Good day Mahini.

Mer. Again delay, I have decided I shall grant an even bigger favor. I now recall an obscure rumor in regard to such a tooth, it's said to be unbreakable, if tis the rumor'd tooth in truth. There is one way to tell if it's the fang does wizard's so enamor. Let's see, wherever did I leave that smithing hammer.

Ryk. So gayly smash away you may, but first let's settle on a price. A wager if you wish, in honor of your favorite vice.

Mer. A wager where I've naught to lose? I shall indulge thee such a game.

Ryk. Then let's begin if all's the same. Ten thousand gold would set me up quite pleasantly.

Mer. Agreed.

Ryk. So readily agreed?

Mer. Agreed, the nonsensical sum I shall not pay would set thee up as king.

Ryk. 'One stair per step as thou dost rise', my poor last master always said; I found his wisdom suspect though, (so I left him for dead.)

Mer. One hundred gold's a mighty step Your Majesty, if truly it's origin can be trusted; it's more likely we barter over some bogus bicuspid.

Ryk. I'll want a court ere I secure the service of a jester; I came to bargain, not be pester'd.

Mer. Because I much admire thy illusions of grandeurity, insanity well season'd with a healthy dash of bold, I'll humor thee by offering one thousand gold.

Ryk. Delivery was better, thy disposition sunnier, yet still I found thy last joke to be funnier.

Mer. Then here's a royal slapper of the knee to last through all the ages that may be: I have gold, you have a tooth.

Ryk. I always knew that fools could sages be in truth. Thy point is taken jester for a king must welcome wisdom when he hears it, I'll come down a thousand for thy wit.

Mer. And I'll reward thy royal introspection, by raising my imaginary offer up to two; made tangible if only it does glow the color of the dragon by the light of two full moons.

Ryk. A knowledgeable fool, for one who's heard but half-forgotten tales.

Mer. It comes from washing breakfast down with wine, the memory returns as the inebriation fails.

Ryk. As barbarous sobriety continues to invade, mayhap the monetary value of so magical a thing will bring to mind where nine thousand gold pieces have been laid; (all shiny and glittering.)

Mer. I thought that we had settled it at two?

Ryk. The voices in thy head perhaps had settl'd it with you.

Mer. Old tales may make such teeth out to be valuable yes, but tales become distorted until truth is but a guess. A legendary lamp without a genie grants no wish, and so I think three thousand an inflated price for such a fairy tale as this. A fortune by all honest reckoning, and three more thousand than I'm guessing thou hast now.

Ryk. More gold will always come to men industrious as us although we know not how. What now I carry in this simple satchel mine is such a find, I doubt that in our lifetimes thou or I will come across another of its kind. Most men can only dream this opportunity we brothers share. I will come down to eight, as courtesy to kin; it's more than fair.

Mer. A sibling courtesy would be to drop thy price to four.

Ryk. Alas but one who shar'd a womb would know it's worth much more. Divinity is priceless and divine is our angelic prize, to go to seven would be quite benevolent in my unbiased eyes.

Mer. My sole devotion is to gambeling; and women of substantial size, so let me be the most devoted man alive and meet a fellow miscreant from birth halfway at five.

Ryk. Divine! Let's come together brother and leave off these foolish tricks. I too will meet thee in the middle between five and seven, which is six.

Mer. Hmmm. We've an agreement then, should this incisor somehow prove the honest article; believe me I shall well examine every part and particle.

Ryk. I'd lose my vast respect for thee if thou didst any less.

Mer. Professionally I confess, this was an unexpected satisfaction. I never thought to find a friend unscrupulous enough to better me fictitiously in a transaction. Were I no only child I would swear we really were of the same blood. Shall we shake hands?

Ryk. My brother nay but we shall hug!

Mer. I see thou found the coin purse from my waist band.

Ryk. Oh this is thine? I'm glad I did discover it before some common swine.

Mer. If thou wouldst kindly and quite slowly hand it back to me?

Ryk. Of course my most perceptive colleague.

[*He does. Merchant tests the weight and looks at Rykel quizzically. Rykel removes a coin from his mouth and drops it in.*]

Mer. (And now to put the tooth unto the test.)

[*Enter Bazeen, unseen.*]

Ryk. Yes line it up, that's it, give it your best.

Mer. I'll harness all my hunger, passion, everything I've got, and focus all upon a very tender spot.

Ryk. Let blood be brought to molten hot and boil as thou pound it heatedly.

Mer. Oh have no fear of that for I shall pummel it repeatedly.

Ryk. Now do the deed and let us seal this deal.

Baz. Whatever are you doing there *Hameel*?

Mer. *Bazeen*, to what do I owe this most unanticipated honor?

Baz. I'm looking for some information.

Mer. I traffic in it.

Baz. Of course you do you mindless rumrunner. Why else would I be- Is this a dragon's tooth I find?

Mer. A canine I believe. That is, the canine of a canine.

Baz. A canine?

Mer. A rather large canine.

Ryk. 'Twas my dog sir, he had a bad disorder as a puppy, and grew to unbelievable proportions, resulting in a famous four-foot femur, forty-four inch feet, and fangular distortions.

Mer. A tragic tale.

Ryk. Indeed one swing could knock a man from off his feet. We were compell'd to put him down for sake of all the sheep, poor dog.

Mer. Was he unruly with the flock?

Ryk. Devour'd ev'ry one, along with Henry, my wife Hellen's favorite hog. I did maintain the tooth as a memento for the shelf, though without hog or sheep or dog we have no means to make a living; my seven children and myself. Their mother, rest her soul, has since departed to be with her ancestors of old. She died last year of, being cold, and I have mouths to feed.

Mer. I'll not deny this flockless shepherd in his time of need. The story of his suffering has struck me like a well thrown dart, within the double bullseye of my tender heart.

Ryk. This charitable merchant offer'd up a modest sum to have it from me as a novelty.

Mer. Indeed I have, well, theoretically.

Ryk. To think I nearly buried it with my dear Heather in the heath.

[*Bazeen draws his blade and brings it down atop the tooth.*]

He suckled well into his second year, which made for brawny bones and most tenacious teeth.

Baz. I claim this for my lord and master.

Mer. Would not a mighty warrior as thyself prefer a wineskin, or perhaps a masculinic statue of a heron carv'd in alabaster?

Baz. I've fallen from his favor as of late, this fang may help alleviate the tension that has risen. Tell me Hameel, not that I care, how did a shifty little con blunder upon a relic beyond rare?

Ryk. The tooth is mine sirrah, it goes where I so chose it.

Baz. You'll guard your tongue or lose it.
Ryk. [*Pulls dagger.*] Hah! What poor fool seeks to part me from my prize?
Mer. He is a wizard's champion.
Ryk. Oh my. [*Pretends he only meant to clean his nails with dagger.*] Forgive me my impertinence most noblest of, noble lords. It seems that fate has brought us here today so let's speak no deceitful words. The truth is thou arriv'd in time to save this honey-tongued merchant from my sword. A dragon's tooth this is, a fine one you can see, twould be my honor to accept an offer from an honest man as thee.
Baz. It's my tooth now, but breathe on it and die.
Ryk. 'Tis clear thou art as much a man of violence as am I. We fire forged warlike peers, whom none would turn their back on without fear, must stick-
Baz. I search for trav'lers three, quite out of place in our society, for they hail from *Natiro*, recent fled most likely seeking refuge. An aged man a woman and a girl, use all your eyes and ears Hameel for if you find them I will be most grateful. My master's purse will share my gratitude.
Ryk. (I sense a softening of attitude.) I've seen these travelers thou seek, oh wealthy and determin'd lord, and even with them did I speak, of which I'll tell thee for the same reward; a pittance surely from thy master's horde.
Baz. Speak dog.
Ryk. A deal should first be struck, as trader's do.
Baz. Our deal is tell me what you know or I will murder you.
Ryk. I do believe we've met our match in bargaining.
Mer. Our better brother, I'd swear it on the grave of our dear mother.
Ryk. I met these good folk on a mountain slope west of Garban. Some friends of yours?
Baz. I'm sent to kill them.

Ryk. Excellent, they had an ill-begotten look about them. I journey'd to the mountain with my manservant, to slay a dragon who had grown most foul. When my courageous squire became crush'd, the dragon then, to honor him, I thoroughly disbowl'd, then wrenched this relic free as was my right, and went to seek a buyer that I might provide a nest egg for my fearless fallen friend's poor family.

Baz. I thought you were a shepherd.

Ryk. A shepherd and a sometime hero, who prefers false modesty o're braggadocious bold bravado. When came I on these most unwholesome marshlanders, the dark was swift approaching. They tried enticing me to share a drink and camp with them, but I could tell their purposes were banditry and poaching. Declin'd I both their company and likely poisen'd flagon; but did divine that they desir'd discourse with the dragon. So now thou knowst how honestly I came by this memento, and why I am so loathe to let it go. To me it is more memory than monetary gain which in thy, meaty hands thou hold.

Mer. It's still not worth ten thousand gold.

Baz. A shepherd hero hound and fool, I may have use for such a versatile tool. What are you call'd that I may heel my newest dog?

Ryk. *Rykel* good sir.

Baz. Then let us see *Rykel* with many tales to tell, if there is any truth to your prolific monologue. Convey me to this mountain and locate their trail. A rich reward awaits you if you do not fail. I have a near unlimited supply of gold if that is what you crave. You just might live to see some, if you are a helpful slave.

Ryk. A hero can bought if they are wise; too many cling to morals and refuse to compromise. Where're we wonder I am thine for now new master, I would even share the burden of the tooth with thee, that we might travel faster.

Baz. It shall be kept about my waist, where you can cast your gaze and salivate. That should keep you from straying when the fire burns low and hours grow late. [*Tosses the merchant a coin-purse.*] We were not here.

Mer. Who speaks?

Baz. I long for songs and laughter as of late; my master has a way of murdering the minstrels I accumulate. I would hear more of your embellish'd deeds as we do pass the time. I don't suppose you can deliver meter'd tales in rhyme?

Ryk. (A modern audience may think that was a travesty, but surely even ears bombarded with one-liners might become accustom'd to iambic poetry.)

Baz. Amuse me and I shall keep thee alive, betray me and I'll boil thee…

Ryk. Alive? Oh very well, it's clear your own attempts at rhyming are contriv'd.

Baz. [*Takes Rykel by the ear.*] Come jack of many made-up trades, it's time to heed thy master's call.

[*Exit Bazeen with Rykel.*]

Mer. Farewell dear brother. (It does appear I am the better in a bargain after all.)

[*Exeunt.*]

Act II, Scene 3

[Enter Melsyne, Drond, Quick, Ekinroy on crutches.]

Ekin. However in the treeless marsh, with timber hard to come upon, didst thou develop such a useful art? These wooden legs amaze me Noble *Drond*.
Dro. The islands do boast forests lakes and even mountains, nothing so expansive as these lofty spires. We waste no art on statues domes or less than nat'ral water fountains, rather hone our skills to help our land entire.
Ekin. Thou art a handy man to have at hand.
Dro. Our party's stronger when we all can stand.
Mel. The shaft is hick'ry, cane the lashing, flexible and tough.
Quik I pray the Thoughts it is enough.
Ekin. I would one day see thy fair home my friend.
Dro. Thou mayest do as thou dost choose, at journey's end. At present hunger calls and air is damp.
Mel. I would speak with the knight alone ere we make camp.
Dro. We shall await thee then, with all the difficult work done.

[Exit Drond, Quik.]

Ekin. What words woulds't thou have for me lady were not fit for everyone?
Mel. Do not assume I mean to speak of pleasantries. *[She draws her sword.]* Thy skills must be kept sharp whe'er fight thee on one foot or on thy knees.

[Ekinroy drops one crutch and pulls his sword. They spar until Ekinroy stumbles.]

Ekin. I thank thee for the practice against expert-wielded steel, that I may better be equipp'd to help defend us should we come under attack ere I am heal'd.

Mel. There is another type of hurt that does not heal the way of flesh and bone. If thou wouldst let me be a friend, I would see that thou dost not suffer on thine own. For only time and council heal the matters of the heart, and thou but recently receiv'd such blows could rend the staunchest heart apart.

Ekin. A friend as thee *Melsyne,* would mighty welcome be. I long have known Sir *Gyle* to be, flaw'd, perhaps I should have never trusted him, but never did I dream the king's friendship a fraud, or that I could not trust fair *Gwendolyn.*

Mel. If I may ask friend *Ekinroy*, how didst thou come to know her?

Ekin. I saw her in the employ of the Sword and Strumpet. A simple serving girl, yet something in her bearing made me think that she was more. In her I spied the makings of a noble lady, but little did I know the horizontal nature that would keep her from ascending far, ere she would drop back down on territory more familiar.

Mel. To lose someone in any way requires time to grieve, for lover's lost or for a slaughter'd family. Believe me for within a year I have known both of these. The monster that we hunt did take my mother and my father, and war before did claim my lover.

Ekin. I swear to bring thy family what small peace that vengeance may provide, and only wish I could bring back thy love from with the Thoughts where he resides.

Mel. Where she resides, my *Chrystalina* with her golden eyes.

Ekin. A lucky lady then, when she was still alive, to have a love as thee when with the living she did still reside.

Mel. How long wert thou betroth'd to, she whose loss is fresh?

Ekin. I'd known her for the better part of two full weeks before I did embark upon my quest. My mother, rest her soul, taught me to trust in others with an open heart, but when she died so died all wisdom she had further to impart.

Mel. At least the trail to your betrayals was bedeck'd with good intent. Thou art a decent man, and so I must repent. The one you seek to slay for us is no sadistic simpleton, but nothing less than-

Ekin. It matters not-

Mel. Shut up. He is a wizard's champion.

Ekin. But that would mean-

Mel. Thy life is forfeit on his death. Grandfather did not wish to make it known, but I can no more hold my breath. He will be furious at first, but I shall speak with him and he will see that we should never have so trick'd thee.

Ekin. Thou needst not say a word to that old man,
And I'll not let on that I know his plan.
I've donn'd the mask of those are as the dead,
Expecting ne'r again to see my home,
What matter by which monster I am bled?
No longer have I home where I would go.
Through combat's carnage, dragon's fiery breath,
Ne'r have I fled from fear of mine own death.
I'll not turn tail when bound as now I am,
But slay this churlish wizard's champion,
And let the wizard take me if he can.
Drond wants me gone well I say let it be,
May my unmoving corpse bring him delight

Should he the sight live long enough to see.
Mel. What foolishness is this I find in thee?
That thou wouldst give thy life so easily.
I thought to help thee through a tender patch,
And lend a friendly shoulder if I could,
But now I question if the plans you hatch
Are born of sheer stupidity or good.
Thy heart at least I thought was passing pure
Yet now I've cause to reassess thy failures.
Tell me in truth why you slew *Monwyrm* knight,
For glory gold or simply for the fight?
Why choose so magical a beast to duel?
Have you a decent reason to relate?
Or did your people simply need a fool
And you were but the biggest they could bait.
I ask again–
Ekin. I was but eight when *Monwyrm* slew my kin,
And left me orphan'd in a burning field.
I went to feed the horses in their pen,
While in the house my fam'ly fast was seal'd.
The fire that took them had no time to spread,
Before the barn was also set alight,
So through the field and t'ward our home I fled,
With timbers crashing round me in the night.
The hay b'ing wet, refus'd to burn at first,
And when I saw that no one had surviv'd,
Acknowledging at last the very worst
I fin'lly hunker'd down in it to hide.
Bones crunch'd behind me, our dead livestock,
The dragon took his time with all our flock.
We gladly would have given sacrifice,
As had before when he was in the sky,
But, we were, unprepar'd.
Mel. Enough. Forgive the words I spoke in haste. We are
the same.

[*She embraces him, lingering slightly after.*] Apparently I'm not the only one who wishes to converse with thee. [*Toward Quik offstage.*] Be sure you make it back to camp in safety.

[*Exit Melsye.*]

[*Enter Quik.*]

Quik She's good.

Ekin. Thou hast a subtle step young *Quik*, I am not easily surpris'd.

Quik I think thou wert somewhat pre-occupied. You should have kiss'd her, might have miss'd your chance.

Ekin. What's that?

Quik Oh nothing. My subtlety was born of stocking prey, and disuse wears ability away. What will you do now that you know the truth? About the prey you swore to slay I mean.

Ekin. I have not had the time to think it through.

Quik It's too bad you're not quick, (like me.) Were me I would be headed for the sea by now believe, that's what I'd do. But knights are touchy 'bout such things I've heard, is there not some strange code that causes you to keep your word?

Ekin. 'Twas in the oath of knighthood given at my accolade.

Quik Yeah that. A little inconvenient don't you think?

Ekin. What is a person does not keep the promises they made?

Quik Alive for one, so they can tell the truth again to counter the deceit.

Ekin. I don't believe-

Quik You think my sister's pretty?

Ekin. She is compassionate, with honesty and deep humility.

Quik Humility? You don't yet know *Melsyne*.

Ekin. She has a fierceness mingl'd with a grace I've seldom seen.

Quik On that we can agree, she sometimes scares the Thoughts right out of me. You sparr'd impressively with her I'll say, at least for having but a single working leg. What thought you of the way she wields a blade?

Ekin. Precise, and strong, yet elegant when flowing form to form, and I think it is less than proper we're discussing this without her.

Quik Propriety's important to a knight?

Ekin. 'Tis tantamount.

Quik That's not the mounting I'd say was important to Sir *Gyle*.

Ekin. I'm sorry thou endur'd that sight.

Quik Oh I walk'd in once on *Melsyne* when I was but thirteen.

Ekin. Let's make our way to camp, I have a sword to clean.

Quik Can I ask questions on the way?

Ekin. Could I thy questions in some way waylay?. One wonders where they come from of a sudden.

Quik 'Twas all that I could do to breathe before, my lungs are fin'lly free once more. Thank all the Thoughts for grandpa's whittling, I love to learn new things; do you whittle?

Ekin. But very little.

Quik What do you like to do for fun?

Ekin. Amusement never had I time to focus on.

Quik *Melsyne* enjoys the hunt, and tying knots, she makes the finest fletching on the island; she poaches feathers sometimes but is never caught. She's always making sure her blades are sharp, and now and then she finds a random fight to start; espeshly when she's had too much to drink.

Ekin. Best not discuss her while she is not here I think.

Quik I love to talk about her when she's not around, what else are younger siblings for? It's not like I said anything profound, or told you of the times her temper got the best of her.
Ekin. I won't believe *Melsyne–*
Quik I heard her laying into you, so you know what I mean. I've seen her send men running for their lives, while seeking refuge from the wrong end of her knives.
Ekin. How many knives does she; no never mind.
Quik Four.
Ekin. Really?
Quik No five. Is it much farther to your mender friend?
Ekin. A few more days, tomorrow you can ask again.
[Exeunt.]

[Enter Melsyne.]

Mel. (The knight's an honest fool as all can see), but far the bigger fool is me.

[Exeunt.]

Act II, Scene 4

*[Enter Medias, gazes into the distance, closes eyes and
tilts head back.]*

[Enter Loren.]

Lor. Do pardon me the interruption. Thou hast some
vis'tors at the gate.
Med. A fickle stream is time that for no one will wait.
Your name is *Loren* is it not?
Lor. Why yes great master.
Med. *Medias* thou mayst call me when we're not around
the others. I've heard the Thoughts favor to thy ear. Was
Their influence that which led you here?
Lor. I hear Their whispers sometimes when I pray. If I
can concentrate, betimes I understand the words they say.
Med. A potent healer thou couldst be one day. I've also
heard thou hast a lovely singing voice.
Lor. I like to sing, sir *Medias* sir.
Med. Just *Medias*. Wouldst thou then bless me with a
song of thine own choice?
Lor. Most happily. *[Closes eyes and breaths deep. Sings
hymnal style.]*

First came the Orb of Unity,
Great Mind bound for eternity.
All was thought and all was one,
Destin'd to be shared 'by none.
Shatter'd into endless night,
Shards of thought that made the light.
Many from a single source,

Sent into the void by force.
Bound by hope they float above,
Searching for a perfect love.

[Subtle change to an eerie chant.]

Neglected ones who stand apart,
Faithless in the human heart.
Bringing death and bringing war,
Longing to be whole once more.

Med. Stop! Where did you learn those last four lines?
Lor. I-I don't know. Sometimes the words just come to mind.
Med. Thou hast a great and terrifying gift, and must be very cautious of those voices in the air adrift. The jealous ones may whisper just as well, and thou canst not put stock in what they tell. Now run along, thou hast delivered thy news.
[Exit Loren.]

(What monstrous trouble brews, when jealous thoughts seek little ones with ears to bend, and Great Thoughts ask a mender to betray a friend.)
[Enter Ekinroy, Melsyne, Quik.]

Med. [*Without turning.*] My morning meditation said thou'd come, and trouble would be traveling with thee. [*Turns to travelers.*] What new harm to thyself hast thou now done? It's not been long enough for thee to have a family.
Ekin. *Medias,* my dear mentor and a dearer friend, and still perceptive as thou've always been. These folk did save me from a slow and painful death. *Melsyne,* and

Quik, along with *Drond* their elder kin; because of them I still draw breath.

Med. Thou hast my thanks, but there should be one other.

Mel. Our grandfather awaits outside the city gates.

Quik He thinks you are a witch doctor.

Med. I see. How didst thou manage to achieve this latest injury?

Ekin. So much the same as long ago; I pick'd a fight with a much larger foe.

Med. I caution'd better care if I recall, the final words I told thee ere I left, though I suspected thou'd ignore them one and all for always knew of fear thou wert bereft. Strong as thou art, invincible thou'rt not; that thou must learn to save thee from thyself the lesson I had hop'd was taught.

Ekin. When first I landed at the orphanage, *Medias* shelter'd me beneath friendly wing, until the gift began to manifest and my good friend was forc'd by fate to flee.

Med. The great ones grant this power I possess, and also wisdom in their words upon the wind. I heard thou fin'lly slew old *Monwyrm.*

Ekin. Yes.

Med. They also gave me insight on the trouble thou art in.

Quik Grandfather might be right.

Med. An answer to a single question waits, a question ask'd of me that I'll relay, an earthly query or of matters strange. Take time, and think on it whilst we address that leg. Lie down my friend, and brace thyself. I've gain'd in skill since we were young, but bones don't knit together easily, so place this bit of rope between thy teeth that thou dost not bite through thy tongue. [*Medias places hands on Ekinroy's broken leg, concentrates.*]

Quik Is something s'ppos'd to happen now?

Mel. Shhhh.
Quik I don't see any-
Mel. Shhhh.

[*Ekinroy and Medias both inhale sharply, rigid in pain as the bone mends.*]

Mel. Please stop, you're hurting him!

[*Ekinroy and Medias exhale together, nearly collapsing. After a moment, Ekinroy stands and tests his leg.*]

Ekin. Thy skill amazes me my dearest friend. Is there no ill thy powers cannot mend?
Med. The power is not mine but of the thoughts, it's only through their will that miracles are wrought. A careful question must be queri'd still, ere we may see completion of their will.
Ekin. I know not even where I should begin, for I have lost all longing for the laying of my path.
Mel. How might a mortal slay a wizard's champion? and not be subject to their master's wrath.
Med. A selfless query else I am mistaken. To take such life and not have thine own taken. [*Methius tilts back his head, closes eyes, listening to voices on the wind.*] No living soul may challenge such a one, without the fear of swiftest retribution; no one, that is, except another wizard's champion. It cannot merely be coincidence that recently I came to know a mage, who struck me in his comely countenance a conjurer quite affable and sage. A drawing shows location of his keep; by thoughts decree he left it here with me. [*Hands map to Ekinroy.*] With passage through a much neglected path, thou canst arrive in under three days time.

Mel. I never have known fate to work so fast, the
Thoughts must truly keep thee in their eye.
Med. Naught but a humble conduit am I. Now thou must
go though I would have thee stay, the import of thy quest
brooks no delay. The wizard's crumbling castle looms
above a crooked stream.
Ekin. No words can capably convey what thy help
means.
Med. It may be he's expecting all of you, so well in tune
with great events is he. Farewell until we meet again.
Ekin. Farewell dear friend.

[Exeunt, manet Medias.]

Med. (Perception's edge is where divinities will lurk,
coincidence our simple minds perceiving them at work.) I
cannot know why Great the Thoughts would wish for
sending thee and thine so unprepar'd into an ambush.
Forgive me friend of journey's past, I pray the path
thou'rt on be not thy last.

[Exeunt.]

Act III, Scene 1

[*Enter Bazeen, Rykel.*]

Baz. From round those rocks we can surprise with ease.
Whor. *Blard*, don't just tie the horses to a tree with rope.
Blard But master said–
Whor. To make a proper picket line you pecker-lacking dope!
Ryk. When thou suggested bolstering our ranks, I had not pictur'd quite the cream of the Irnori drunk tanks.
Baz. They're desp'rate men who never will be miss'd, such are the type I prefer to enlist. Since none may slaughter me they're really just accessories.
Ryk. We could at least have hose'd them down, my nose has not known peace ere we left town.
Baz. My master has a tendency to thin my ranks at will, so I prefer retainers I won't miss if he decides to kill; but no offense of course.
Ryk. Of course; I am deplorable, I only live because thou find my lies adorable.
Baz. You do though make me laugh, there's something to be said for that.
Ryk. Good laughter is like gold unto the soul they say.
Baz. That makes no sense.
Ryk. It did inside my head, but wit is tied to senses and the smell has made my senses dead.

[*Enter Whorlick and Blard.*]
Whor. What now me-lord?
Baz. We wait.

Ryk. And what do we wait for, oh leader great?
Baz. Our much elusive quarry has been found.
Ryk. Was I asleep on horseback when we track'd them down?
Baz. My master's words have echoed in my mind.
Ryk. Thy senses too have been affected by this air unkind.
Baz. It is a bond you would not understand, but know that these Natiran's here are bound, another travels with them, some fortuneless companion they have found.
Ryk. Thy word Is good enough for me, besides I have six thousand reasons not to leave. Warlock-
Whor. *Whorlick*.
Ryk. Blurb-
Whor. Ee's *Blard*.
Ryk. Spread out, tis better when we're far apart.

[*They spread out in wait. Quik groans.*]

Blard Someone comes.
Baz. Do not be seen until I spring the trap, then let no one escape beyond our back.

[*They hide. Quik groans again.*]

Dro. By all the Thoughts whatever is the matter?
Quik Why can't the mainland be, flatter?
[*Enter Melsyne, Ekinroy, Drond, Quick.*]

Ekin. The climax of this trail is quick to come.
Quik It's all downhill from there?
Dro. That's what it means young one. We swift approach the highpoint of the stair.

Quik That doesn't mean there's no more rises. It might go down and up and down and up as many times as this mountain devises.

Mel. 'Tis more downhill than not, if that does suit thee better.

Quik A better definition than the other.

Dro. Thy quest for perfect definitions is unhealthy.

Quik I would be rich one day; and those are dumb are rarely wealthy.

Baz. [*Steps out to block their path*.] That dream will die today along with you, no coin to call your own and far from home. Throw down your steel for nothing can you do, it is decided that you may no longer roam.

> [*Whorlick and Blard step out as though to block any retreat*.]

I do regret what happen'd with thy kin, and promise if thou help to make this quick, I will not let the same occur again, but make thy deaths as painless as the pricking of a pin. I've more associates within the trees, it's easier for all if thou discard thy weapons and go willing to thy knees. Hmmm. It seems you do not know me after all, or you would surely cower ere you fall.

Ekin. We know thou art *Bazeen*, a Wizard's Champion, but know that I fear not thy master's retribution. Thy fight is not with these fair folk but I instead, Sir *Ekinroy* a knight of *North Kalas*; who by my kingdom's law is deem'd already dead.

> [*They fight. Bazeen is disarmed, Melsyne stops Ekinroy from killing him. Whorlick, Blard, Rykel flee*.]

Baz. You will regret that e're you join'd this fight, knight.

[*Melsyne knocks Bazeen unconscious.*]

Dro. The fiend has life; you have betray'd us knight.
[*Draws weapon.*]
Mel. 'Twas I who caus'd the knight to stay his hand,
A choice by which unwavering I stand.
Medias found a path providing peace
If thou thy hatred of this knight release,
For if thou treat a life so carelessly,
Thy enemy's already beaten thee.
Bazeen shall not again his freedom gain
Until the knight a mage as master takes,
And then his life Sir *Ekinroy* shall claim,
When he on our behalf a challenge makes.
Dro. What foolishness so simply given voice, as though
a preordain'd conspiracy. Apparently I have no prudent
choice, this man has turn'd my only kin against me.
Ekin. I've seen this sealed bag and know that bulge, will
it a wanted secret here divulge? [*Reveals dragon's tooth.*]
Can there be doubt the Thoughts are with us friends? We
can but walk the path they set until it ends.

[*Exeunt.*]

Act III, Scene 2

[Child #1 enters, brandishing a wooden sword, Child #2 sneaks up behind and attacks with their own stick-weapon.]

Ch 2. Hah!
Ch 1. Shhh! This is the wizard's keep.
Ch 2. How deep dost think the moat?
Ch 1. Deep.
Ch 2. I nothing fear, I'll cross the bridge and then attack!
Ch 1. You're on your own then, I am going back.
Ch 2. Our mother says the blood of kings runs through our veins.
Ch 1. If so it'd be a shame to lose it down the wizard's drains.
Ch 2. He'll tremble 'fore our measurable might,
our noble blood does come to claim our right.
By this ancestral sword of strongest wood,
I'll claim this keep as our ancestors, would.
No magic conjuration shall deter,
Nor man nor beast can hope to hinder me,
If come we 'cross this wicked conjurer,
Then he shall flee from our most righteous fury,
Come sibling!
[Enter Bazeen, bound and gagged. He falls to his knees with a groan.]

Ahhh! Flee! Flee!
[Exit Child #1 and Child #2.]

[*Enter Melsyne, Ekinroy, Quik, Drond.*]

Quik This castle gives me creeps, I swear I heard the shriek of some unearthly apparition.

Mel. 'Tis but the next leg of our expedition.

Ekin. The wind plays tricks on all unwary ears, but those are just need not give in to fears. The thoughts have led us to this fated place, and so do guide us in our ev'ry pace. When I return reviling murd'rous foe, we shall meet fairly and trade blow for blow. If all goes well I will be back ere long; then let the Thoughts decide whose cause is right, and whose is wrong.

Mel. Thou shalt not go alone, I'll be with thee.

Quik If she goes then I surely will go too.

Ekin. Within these walls may lie some danger yet unseen.

Mel. Precisely why we mean to go with you. Thou'd have to bind our hands as well to keep us from these hidden halls.

Quik We've travell'd over hill and under dell, though mostly over hill, and would not let thee leave us here when danger calls.

Ekin. I cannot let thee.

Mel. Our actions are not thine to contradict.

Dro. Mark well with poachers and unruly pets, when poison 'ssures into the trap they're trick'd, the poachers may be caught in their own nets; my money says this is an empty den.

Ekin. Our pris'ner must stay guarded here without, for I'll not burden they who dwell within with bus'ness only we must be about.

Dro. You have my word that I will guard him well, until you've sold what lies you've come to sell.

Mel. We shall return grandfather, have no fear, upon the locket that thou wear, I swear. This villain will regret the actions e'er did lead us to this duty driven dragon slayer.

[Exeunt, manet Bazeen and Drond.
Bazeen makes muffled noises until Drond removes his
gag.]

Baz. My gratitude to you for that is vast.
Dro. Speak wisely for these words may be your last.
Baz. You don't believe he'll really try to kill me this
time do you? What'ere he claims he rightly fears my
master. I simply was caught unprepar'd when first we
drew, for him to try again would be disaster. Besides I
doubt they shall return at all, your kin so clearly in his
knightly thrall. You know'st of what I speak oh wizen'd
fellow; they follow him like trained hounds may do.
[Enter Rykel sneakily, a dagger drawn.]

Before thy face they placate thee I know;
Behind thy back they scorn and ridicule.
My master can be cruel, as thou hast seen,
But I do swear that if thou giv'st me flight,
I will petition him for amnesty,
And then return and rid thee of the knight.
And too I'll thee reward with hordes of gold,
That thou mayst spend e'en ere the knight is cold.
Relieve me of my bonds and tell them this;
That I surpris'd thee when thou turnst thy back,
A kick unto thy tender temple swift,
And all thou saw beyond was darkest black.
Though we will ne'er friends, the past is past,
Together, for the children, we'll assure a future that will
last.

[Drond pulls a knife as if to cut bonds, then places it at
Bazeen's throat.]

Dro. No one intoning throat so worthy's been as thine of swiftest silencing. Did you think flower'd words would draw me like a bee when if I could I'd censor them eternally? I gave my word that I would guard you well, the word for honest men more sacred than the breath, and but a fool would slay the foulest foe when it means certain death. The wizard that you serve will feel you die, is this the truth you would have us believe?

Baz. Oh aye, it is the honest truth assuredly, an unearthly demise of magic born awaits the poor assassin slaughters me.

Dro. Then to his word I'll hold the knight, and he shall spill your final blood; but first I'll cut you, maim you, see you bleed, and leave him nothing but a dying husk that he may squish as simply as a bug. For what care I if thou hast eyes, a nose, a tongue? These things belong to men with long to live, and you have not.

[Rykel knocks Drond unconscious from behind.]

Baz. My funny little thief, thy timing is a precious thing.

Ryk. It's lucky the old man had so much wind to work his beak, if not for such a villain's monologue I'd not have had the time it took to sneak.
(For those are set on proper torturing,
Will not with words assault a captive's ear,
But rather shear an ear and make them scream;
Description only causes so much fear.
They'll not drone on and on about their crime
As in some heighten'd language play
For only reason has a proper place in rhyme;
Much better to say what they have to say
In one quite dumb and dry iconic line.)

Baz. Most timely interference either way, thy actions warrant increase in thy pay.

Ryk. Considering my pay was watch and salivate, this seems a good time to negotiate.

Baz. First cut me free and freely may we talk, your loyalty will nothing be for naught.

Ryk. If barter we before unburden'd by these bonds thou be, a better bargain it may guarantee, for me.

Baz. I'm in no disposition–

Ryk. Nor in any position.

Baz. But name thy price and have this nonsense done.

Ryk. Our last negotiation was not nearly so much fun. I'd ask for gold, but far too weighty would the asking be, so something smaller then that I might carry easily. Let's see. It must be valu'ble and portable; there was an object that I once possess'd in truth, before it was remov'd by methods forcible. I do believe it was–

Baz. The dragon's tooth. Of course, thou can remove it from Sir Whats-his-face's corpse.

Ryk. The nameless knight did best thee once before.

Baz. A lucky strike for I misjudged his skill, which only means I'll more enjoy the kill.

Ryk. I fear I'll need assurance for this crime, he has a habit of escaping death, I left him 'neath a dragon once upon a time and somehow he surviv'd it's heft; he was my master once I must admit.

Baz. Hast ever been a master you did not desert?

Ryk. Not yet, but make the last one die and you may be the first.

Baz. What apt assurance would appease thee?

Ryk. You plan to find more men I would presume?

Baz. I do.

Ryk. Let me decide them then, and we'll our partnership resume.

Baz. Agreed.

[Rykel cuts Bazeen's bonds.]

I hope my master takes a shine to thee my clever thief,
thy death would cause me some small grief.
Ryk. Thy forward manner grows on me as well. So come
my oldest and most trusted friend, our troubles swift
approach their happy end, we've but a knight to kill, a
tooth to sell.

[*Exeunt.*]

Act III, Scene 3

[Enter Ekinroy, Melsyne, and Quik.]

Quik Such vari'd oddities I've never seen. Is that a giant's skull? His entrails may be in a jar beneath.

Ekin. *Medias* would not send us into peril, we are as safe as fish within a barrel.

Quik What if the wizard doesn't like your friend? What if he blasts us to oblivion?

Ekin. Our souls will join with the Thoughts in grace, while our corporeality does fade.

Quik What if he holds us all in limbo for a thousand years and when we wake the world has chang'd?

Ekin. We'll grow accustom'd to the way the new world is arrang'd.

Quik What if he levitates our eyeballs from our sockets and then sends them out into the atmosphere, so we can view the wonders of the universe while our vacated bodies remain here? What if–

Mel. What if he feasts on little girls who ask too many random questions?

Quik My mind can find more fav'rable receptions.

Spur. Who dares approach the knowing seeing hearing mighty master of illusive augury!? Speak swiftly or the wizard will unleash his fury!

Ekin. Reveal yourself if we would speak, for hiding shall not net the answers that you seek.

[Enter Spurion.]

My name is *Ekinroy Carthagian*, and I would meet the wizard *Spurion*.

Spur. Ha! And why should he be bother'd by the likes of thee?

Ekin. I come to offer-

Spur. He knows why you have come, Sir *Ekinroy*, with *Quik Melsyne* and *Drond*, dos't think he does not see all matters in eternity? He would have thee complete a single task if entry to his awesome service thou dost ask.

Ekin. What task?

Spur. [*Draws sword.*] If thou canst best this blade, oh would-be wizard's errand boy, then in his service thou shalt be, the newest toy in his much-sought employ.

Ekin. [*Draws.*] Prepare thee then relentless mouth of *Spurion*, for thou shouldst know that I did–

Spur. Slay a fearsome dragon? Yes yes we're all aware that you can use your steel, but you'll need wits to live through this ordeal.

[*Ekinroy tries to attack, but Spurion's blade mirrors every motion.*]

Ekin. Impossible, that blade has been bewitch'd.

Spur. Did you expect some common backyard duel? You offer service to a mighty mage and so must prove you are no muscl'd fool. A riddle then if fealty you would find, how might you win this battle, with your mind?

[*Ekinroy punches him. Spurion loses his sword and stumbles back. Ekinroy steps warily on the sword.*]

Ekin. You are disarm'd sirrah, depart or be of better help.

Spur. By all the sacred shrines of long-forgotten Seridu, thou were suppos'd to turn thy blade upon thyself.

Ekin. Why would I do so foolish of a thing?
Spur. 'Twas meant to be a lesson in humility.
Ekin. I'll not abide some surly servant's rule, now show us to your master without further ridicule.
Spur. I'm am the master that thou seek, (they all have figur'd that by now).
Ekin. Then prove it with some magic conjuring.

[*Spurion gestures and Ekinroy is disarmed.*]

Quik Wow.
Spur. [*Chanted with all available voices.*]

> *Behold the wild wanderer,*
> *Immortal born at dawn of time,*
> *An ally to all nat'ral beasts,*
> *A friend of humble human kind.*
>
> *The bane of ancient giant seeds,*
> *And maker of almighty kings,*
> *Who did the noblest of deeds,*
> *By giving up his ruling rings.*
>
> *An ageless mystic of pure thought,*
> *Whose loyalty could not be bought,*
> *Protects the minds of you and I,*
> *And tam'd the lord of all the sky.*
>
> *The right hand of the Father true,*
> *Protects against the tricks they try,*
> *Who will not let the jealous through,*
> *Though evil glint in ev'ry eye.*

Ekin. [*Kneels.*] Forgive my doubt.
Quik Are we about to die?

Spur. No questions out of you young miss; I have not
eaten any children since my breakfast.
Mel. Forgive us for thou art not what we were expecting.
Spur. A long grey beard and flowing robes I am
suspecting? Fear not, thou hast prevail'd against my test,
though I profess, thy methods were much less, cerebral
than I would have guess'd. A bargain is a bargain though,
if promis'd by the wind or etch'd in stone. [*Holds his
sword aloft*.]
Here by the sacred blade of Taren Garth,
Forg'd in the mountain bears it's maker's mark,
I hereby strip thee of all titles old,
And dub thee champion of *Spurion*,
As by the Thoughts above was long foretold.
Rise, my champion.

[*When Ekinroy rises, the mask of the dead is gone.*]

Quik What happen'd to your face.
Spur. A simple spell and easy to erase. We share a bond
unbreakable my friend, and I'll require much of thee
before thy service ends. Thy time for now is all thine
own, if I'm in need of thee, thou'lt know.
Ekin. A debt I owe that now must be repaid.
Spur. Well then, the Thoughts watch over thee and give
thee aid.
[*Exeunt, manet Spurion.*]

(A worthy champion, and more; a perfect means to settle
an old score.) Where did I put that pain-relieving root?
The test perhaps was not so well thought through.

[*Exeunt.*]

Act III, Scene 4

*[Enter Mercenaries marching in file. They stop as one
and turn out.
Enter Captain, Rykel, Bazeen.]*

Cap. My men are disciplin'd as you can see,
accomplish'd in the art of war.
Ryk. We do believe thee Captain Slashity, but we need
killers as I said before. Will they obey commands that to
the common man might seem, obscene?
Cap. They follow orders, if that's what you mean.
Ryk. Would they attack a woman? um, hypothetic'lly of
course.
Cap. If she were wielding weaponry they would resort to
force.
Ryk. And what about a child?
Cap. If some young one was threatening and arm'd.
Ryk. A dog?
Cap. A snarling canine could be harm'd.
Ryk. Would they decapitate domesticated cats?
Cap. Why-
Baz. Enough of that, perhaps we should interrogate the
men, who each have sep'rate tongues on them.
Ryk. What count can claim you crafty warrior, in men
made not so living by thy blade?
Mer 1. Some twelve in total sir, though not all by my
steel so made.
Ryk. Didst thou leave one or two with arrows in their
backs?

Mer 1. I had to strangle one, and brain'd another with the handle of an axe.

Ryk. [*Nods approving.*] And you, why you're a burly one, I'll bet you've split a head or two for fun.

Mer 2. I'll kill for coin as do my brothers. We are professionals, unlike some of the others.

Ryk. Professionals will do as they are told? No matter motive of who holds the gold?

Mer 2. Save for my own life or a trusted fried, there is none that for pay I would not end.

Ryk. Your only mother?

Mer 2. She died when I was young.

Ryk. Your father then?

Mer 2. I heard that he was hung.

Ryk. The fam'ly pet?

[*Bazeen smacks him.*]

Yes-yes, a few more questions and then on our way. You, soldier, to what lengths would you go to earn an ev'ning's pay?

Mer 3. I'd gut a thousand men without remorse to feed my fam'ly for a day.

Ryk. No not this one for his priorities are errant. Be gone; that goes for any other duty-driven parent. These who are left will do just fine. Now pay the man *Bazeen*, whilst I procure some wine.

[*Exeunt*]

Act III, Scene 5

[Enter Ekinroy, Melsyne, Quik.]

Quik The clouds are turning dark.
Mel. Stay on your guard.
Ekin. When rain does come it will fall swift and hard.
Quik How will we know grandfather lives if rain covers his track?
Ekin. Retain thy grief for what is truly lost, maintain belief that we will bring him back; until we've fought till we cannot, we must hold onto hope at any cost.

[Enter Rykel at a run, falls.]

Ryk. Please someone keep me from captivity!
Ekin. *Rykel*? My surly little servant I thought not to see anon?
Ryk. Can fortune fin'lly favor me, and bring to life a master who I thought was gone?
Ekin. Where have you been you wretched little vagabond?
Ryk. Most timeliest of Thoughtful interventions, know I only acted with the best intentions. Such fire and smoke did choke and so I fled, my spirit broke and sure that thou wert dead. But bless the blindest chance that brings thee back, for captive have I been, forc'd to play convincing part of friend. I see the mask is lifted from thy face, thou must have found the tooth pinch'd from my waste?
Ekin. The tooth you took was needless got, for fortune from Garban I garner'd not, but from the company of honest friends my self impos'd exile ends.

Ryk. You have it then, unblemished and whole? Still undiminished from Garban's ritual? Of course, I recognize the pouch.

[Rykel reaches for the pouch, Ekinroy grabs him by the throat.]

Ouch.
Ekin. Of many lessons I have recent learn'd,
Since thrice betray'd by presupposed friends,
Is how another's trust must first be earn'd
Before a meaningful acquaintanceship begin. *[Lets go of Rykel.]*
Ryk. Now!

[Enter Captain and Mercenaries who quickly surround the travelers with swords drawn.]

I did not need your friendship idiot, but only to amuse you till my men were put in place, and since my purpose I did well beget, I'll now enjoy the look upon your face.
Ekin. Unworthy of your mother's love are you, who vainly hop'd to turn a weasel true.
Ryk. Unworthy are you of the wealth you have, so uselessly bestow'd within a bag. To you a trifling trinket for the crown, whilst I would work to spread such wealth around. And why enrich those who are rich already? For honor, duty? Diseases have disabl'd wits for perpetuity.

[Enter Drond bound and gagged, propelled by Bazeen.]
Baz. You play'd that well *Rykel* my little fool, for surely I felt he must murder you; 'twere me I would have certainly if underneath a dragon you'd abandon'd me. A gem I found from you Sir Knight, within this scheming miscreant, had you his talents better put to use, you might

not be in this predicament. Dispose of this old man; you others kneel. Well? Good gold paid I precuring mercenary steel.

[*A mercenary draws sword and approaches Drond.*]

Ekin. Desist, by order of a wizard's champion.
Baz. Continue; no such order have I given.
Ekin. You look upon the champion of *Spurion*, a wizard with no need to hide his name, if any here but harm a single hair upon my head, or those of my companions true, within the week ensuing you'll be dead, this much I absolutely promise you.
Mel. Didst thou not see this possibility my lord?
Baz. It matters not, for I myself still have a sword, and fear no simple knight who would be more. [*Draws sword, moves toward Drond.*]
Èkin. A sword whose poison tip should point to me,
For in my master's name, [*Draws.*] I challenge thee.

[*The mercenaries lower their weapons and step back.*]

Baz. I did not bid thee drop thy guards you fools.
Cap. Though we be paid we must obey some rules. The law itself prevents our intervention, not some weak unrav'ling of our nerve, a clearly stated law in its intention; created by the wizards thou both serve. A lawful challenge between champions is no concern of ours, nor any soldier seeks to live for long, though on my honor sir if thou this man outpower, we shall honor any monetary obligation. If thou dost not survive this fair hostility, what matter to a dead man will it be?
Èkin. Two swords alone shall this dispute decide, behind the butchery of others may a master's hound no longer hide.

Baz. So be it, champion and knight-no-more, for this time I am ready for our fight, you caught me off my guard before, but now you'll feel a real champion's might.

[*They fight. Both receive wounds. They separate for a moment, and Rykel darts in and slashes Ekinroy across the back of the leg. Ekinroy falls to one knee.*]

Baz. How fitting you should bend a bloody knee, before a better champion than thee.
Ekin. [*Rises shakily.*] I would not bow to some murdering knave, though deep within the ground I were already laid.

[*Bazeen attacks relentlessly. Ekinroy fends him off, disarms him, and kicks him to the ground. As Ekinroy begins to advance, Rykel darts forward again.*]

Mel. Behind you!

[*Ekinroy turns, Rykel backs away. Bazeen pulls a dagger from his boot and grabs Melsyne while she is focused on Rykel. Melsyne holds Bazeen's knife hand back.*]

Baz. The noble once-Sir *Ekinroy* would never let a lady die.
Mel. I... am... a... sword maiden... of... Natiro.

[*Melsyne pulls the dagger away and plunges into his gut.*]

Baz. My… master…

[*Melsyne removes the dagger and makes to cut Bazeen's throat. Ekinroy stops her, takes the dagger, and does it himself. Rykel sneaks up behind Ekinroy and grabs hold of the pouch containing the tooth. Ekinroy struggles weakly to hold onto it, Rykel raises his dagger.*]

Ryk. No fool would murder you and risk a wizard's wrath, but surely they won't mind a missing hand.

[*Melsyne mimics throwing a knife. Ekinroy lets go of the pouch containing the tooth. Rykel drops dagger and reaches back to remove Melsyne's bloody knife from his back.*]

Mel. I told you I would kill you if you came near those I love again.

[*Rykel removes the tooth from the pouch.*]

Ryk. Why must the cursed knight forever win? For this I gave my life? It does not sparkle. It does not shine. There is no light, though now the tooth be mine.

[*Rykel dies. Drond stirs.*]

Quik Grandfather!

[*Quik runs to see to Drond as Melsyne sees to Ekinroy. The Mercenaries share a look with their Captain, then draw swords and kneel as one.*]

Mel. What's this?
Cap. Our patron now lies dead, and we have mouths to feed. We'd offer thee our service sir, if thou hast need.

Mel. Why think you he would hire harden'd animals as you?

Cap. We are as hard as is the master we're beholden to. To this one we were bound not out of loyalty, but only out of unemploy'd necessity. A wizard's champion is liken to a king in many lands, and will have need of soldiers with experience to carry out commands. For such as thee would we forgo our going rate, and swear our fealty simply for a master's grace. For we have seen thou art a worthy liege, a master we might follow proud and tall, and ev'ry warrior longs for such prestige; a lord they'd serve when offered no coin at all.

Ekin. I...

Cap. But please my lord, a soldier's life is all we know. We may be forc'd to banditry if no work comes before the snow.

Ekin. Thy words... [*Passes out.*]

Mel. If ever thou wouldst hope to serve him, move him to some drier ground.

[*Exit two mercenaries with Ekinroy.*]

Prepare some cloth for bandages, and then to *Crysin* and *Medias* we are bound.

[*Exit Quik with Drond in tow.*]

You others bury these without delay, then catch us on the trail to *Crysin's* eastern gate.

[*Exeunt.*]

Act III, Scene 6

[Enter Ferryman #1 and Ferryman #2.]

Fer 1. We are the luckiest alive we friends, who thrive within a line of industry the rising sun begins and not till setting ends.

Fer 2. Has time yet come? I am so bor'd that I could sob.

Fer 1. The time is near.

Fer 2. Not near enough, I hate this job.

Fer 1. You've been a ferryman a single moon. Have trust thou must; thoul't learn to love it soon. Till then resume the quiet musings of thy mind. Time takes all troubles far away, so take thy time.

Fer 2. My time is what I waste, for no one at this rate.

Fer 1. But be content, we are well paid to wait.

Fer 2. Well, paid are we, I only wish we were paid well.

Fer 1. Enjoy the sun and suck inside the sultry smell. For nowhere else does marshland meet the sea with such a splash of salty spray against stagnicity, where crashing waves collide with rock and muck, the cries of gulls combine with quack of duck, crustac'ans clatter 'gainst the croak of frog, melodic melodies that mesh among the bog.

Fer 2. Cacophonic catastrophe more like.

Fer 1. Relax, and inspiration soon may strike. A mind meanders in a mist like this, shapes come to life in one's imagination, and barriers erode that would obscure our bliss. A lazy morning find we lucky two within.

Fer 2. It's true I find myself in mourning friend; it started when this job did first begin.

Fer 1. The world's a harsh and unforgiving place, employment's an escape that puts a smile on the face. I am content to throw my stones and dream.

Fer 2. Then dream a ferry moves with water wind or steam, so you can operate it without me, there are exciting places I would be.

Fer 1. What wouldst thou do upon the road to earn thy pay? Alone, afraid, with no one you could trust, expos'd to foreign elements all day; remember that the marshlands have no dust.

Fer 2. I'd visit ever new enticing lands, amassing mighty fortunes by the skill of my two hands!

Fer 1. Why many fortunes I have made in my own time.

Fer 2. What you?

Fer 1. Oh aye; within the journeys of my mind. Such lovers have I known, but rarest beauties all, then up and left them longing for my call. A jester wizard king, a dashing hero have I been, more lives than ten more simple-minded men. Careers relaxing have so much to give, with ev'ry stone I throw another life I live.

Fer 2. Give me one of thy magic wishing stones. Perhaps I too could love this occupation.

[*Ferryman #1 hands them a stone, which they throw.*]

Fer 1. Didst meet a lusty mistress? Topple thrones?

Fer 2. I was an inattentive ferryman.

Fer 1. You've no imagination.
    [*Enter Drond, Quik, Melsyne, Ekinroy.*]

Some passengers approach our sacred site, look lively, and do try to be polite.

Mel. We've made the morning ferry just in time, as shadows start to shrink from rising light.

Dro. It should be gone before the sun so high does climb, but still I will admit that it's a welcome sight. I've long'd for the familiar feel of home, e'en though the mainland, in the end, held more compassion than I could have known.

Mel. Twould not have been so bad to have to wait, with company whose absence soon will heavy lay.

Dro. Thou sav'd this aged fool young champion, in more ways than the noticeable one. Because of thee a better man does live, I would that there were more to thee I had to give.

Ekin. I'll settle for and end to enmities, for such as we, who both at heart crave fairness and equality, should never from this moment strangers be.

Dro. Thou make it sound an honest deal, and yet, I fear I am forever in your debt. You there, ferrymen, when do you depart?

Fer 1. Good morn my ladies, and my lords. [*Clears throat.*]

Fer 2. Good morn my ladies, and my lords. [*Receives an elbow.*] Welcome. This baleful barge [*Another elbow.*], this most phenomenal and swiftly flowing ferry shall depart as soon our fair sun tops yonder pine, good sir.

Fer 1. Pine? Nay I told you yonder fir; we're late!

Dro. A happy mishap, or you'd have an empty boat.

Fer 1. An empty boat or no, when sun is over fir this wood must float. The owners they will not pleas'd, we must make up some time so that our punishment is eas'd. This way and quick!

Quik You know of me?

Fer 1. We'll make our introductions on the journey.

Dro. Be calm, we have goodbyes to make. A taxing quest is ended and a proper leave we must now take.

Fer 1. There is no time!
Fer 2. [*Elbows him.*] Polite.
Fer 1. A few more moments I suppose would be alright.
Mel. Where art thou bound now this bus'ness is done?
Ekin. Again to Crysin on the orders of my master, *Spurion*, there to train King *Eurion's* young son. A reputable post far from Garban, where I would rather not return again.
Mel. I wouldst thou had an old familiar friend in such an unfamiliar place, who could advise and comfort through new challenges thou face.
Ekin. Medias shall advise, as time allows.
Mel. It seems his time is mostly taken by his mender's vows. Much better if thou hadst a friend like me, who oft has long'd for changes in her scenery.
Ekin. My door to all of thee will ever open be.
Mel. What if–
Fer 1. And such a moment that it was, so touching truly, now it's done, let's all aboard the ferry everyone!
Dro. You'll wait sirrah till we are proper parted.
Fer 1. We will be parted from employment if we don't get started.
Dro. Would rather you be parted from your head?
Fer 2. It is a simple question.
Fer 1. We'll wait till thy goodbyes are said.
Dro. A wise decision.
Fer 2. Employment or a head to loose? It pains me that you took so long to choose.
Ekin. Farewell dear *Quik*, mayst thou the answers find to ev'ry question that may cross thy mind.
Quik Farewell good knight, or champion, or any title down the line, a final question though; art thou deaf dumb and blind?
Ekin. Beg pardon?

Quik If you head back to *Crysin* on your own, I'll be convinc'd your head is made of bone.

Ekin. Forgive me for I know not what thou mean.

Quik Would it not be a shorter journey with *Melsyne*?

Ekin. A woman such as she has better things-

Mel. A woman such as she can well decide what her own future brings.

Ekin. Apologies, of course I'd much enjoy thy company.

Mel. A shame the choice has not been offer'd me.

Ekin. Ah…

Dro. (To calmly face a dragon and a wizard's champion, and then to loose the nerve at an expected invitation; 'twas worth the effort dragging him from underneath the dragon just for this.)

Quik (I swear I don't know what she sees in him.)

Ekin. Wouldst thou, *Melsyne*…

Fer 1. A shame he was too shy to ask, now onward with our task. [*Makes ready to leave.*]

Dro. Hold.

Fer 1. We dare not or we'll both be unemploy'd!

Fer 2. Can you not see the customer's annoyed? Forgive me sir, he is an errant rogue with no respect for his position; take all the time thou needst to make this difficult decision.

Ekin. *Melsyne*, together have we conquer'd much, our chance association made us stronger, thy wisdom and companionship I value such, wouldst thou allow me priv'lege of thy company a little longer?

Mel. I would good champion, and thank thee for the invitation; regardless of my family's persuasion. But what of thee grandfather and the farm, wilt thou not be hard-press'd without the extra arm?

Dro. Place not me on my deathbed before time, thy sister and myself shall manage fine, but stag and fish and fowl beware, we hunters do return and all such game is fair.

Quik Do not believe to keep thy lives discreet, if thou do not write frequently I shall have many questions next we meet.

Mel. Please always know, awake or fast asleep, you both will ever be within my thoughts until again your company I keep.

[Melsyne embraces Drond and Quik.]

Fer 2. Is that a tear amongst thy stubble? Oh what a treat.

Fer 1. It's condensation only, which forms when moisture mixes with the heat.

Dro. Come now you two, this ferry won't propel itself.

Fer 2. We're working on that.

Dro. What foolishness. Get to your stations if you value you your health. Can you not see these two are in some need of privacy? Whatever happen'd to your sense of urgency?

[The ferrymen take up their poles and propel the ferry away.]

Fer 2. My friend I finl'y had a dream my own.

Fer 1. Ambitious too, if judging by thy tone.

Fer 2. I wish to be a hero in the bedrock of my soul.

Fer 1. Start smaller friend, 'tis dangerous to daydream while you're handling your pole.

[Exeunt, manet Ekinroy, Melsyne.]

Mel. I fear'd that we might end this quest apart, against the greater wishes of my heart.

Ekin. Forgive, for I did hesitate to force on thee a choice between an unknown future and thy family.

Mel. We don't apologize for near mistakes where I am from.
Ekin. How do they then express remorse for wrongs?
Mel. With action not with words.

**Optional: They kiss, or Melsyne stops Ekinroy's kiss with a finger to his lips.*

Mel. The morning wastes away whilst here we stay, let's take advantage of the light of day, and then procure a wayside nest to rest within, before a brand-new journey we begin.

[*Exeunt.*]

FINIS

PUNCTUATION GUIDELINES

[Based on Original Practice Shakespeare guidelines, for use with all J.L. Davis Original Practice plays.]

Comma=Half stop w/ breath.
Period=Full stop w/ breath. [Mid-line periods in lines of verse should not be treated as a stop.]
Question mark=Full stop w/ breath. [Mid-line question mark in lines of verse should not be treated as a stop.]
Colon=Briefly speed up. [As if to hold someone's attention, not be interrupted, or excited about a new thought.]
Semicolon=Distinct change in thought. [Breath optional.]
Parenthesis=Suggests delivery to audience. [Many other lines may also be played to audience.]

GENERAL NOTES

The iambic rhythm is essential for this play. It is the 'heartbeat' of each character and each character's heartbeat is unique. Together, the heartbeats equal the heartbeat of the play, and as with all living things if the heartbeat stops, the play… dies. The rhythm can almost always be easily found by stressing the second syllable of each line. If a line is not written in iambic, there is a reason ['Real-talk' asides to audience, character is flustered, etc.*]

*Most lines rhyme. It is up to the performer to choose which rhymes are important to emphasize and which should be played down to avoid the language becoming sing-songy.

*If every line of an extended paragraph begins with a capitol letter, it is verse. [*Most verse lines will have 10 beats, soft endings will have 11*.]. If not, it is prose. There are many reasons a character may switch from verse to prose or vice versa, often within a single monologue. It is usually a simple change in emotion or tactic, but it is very important to find, or create, that reason for yourself when reading/performing the character.

*Words that end in 'ed' always receive a separate beat for the 'ed', but words that naturally receive a separate beat for an 'ed' ending do not receive an extra beat.

*Words that contain a non-possessive apostrophe are truncated, or contracted, removing a beat or beats. [*Example: Possessed=3 beats. Possess'd=2 beats.*]

*The fourth wall does not exist. The audience should be treated as a member of the cast as long as they, as a whole and/or individually, do not become uncomfortable. Excessive commotions in the audience should by tactfully acknowledged and perhaps remarked on in character and treated as part of the show. The same is true of excessive disturbances. The idea, as always, is to pull the audience into the world of the play and keep them there. If they wish to be completely ignored by performers, they most assuredly have a television at home.

Mahalo!

Plays by J.L Davis:
The Dragon's Tooth
Mryadawn
The Book of Nebia
Witch Queen of the Isle
Little Birds

Novels by J.L. Davis:
Fall of Crysin (Book I of the Irrillania Chronicles)
Ashes of Crysin (Book II of the Irrillania Chronicles)

Coming soon:
Blood of Crysin (Book III of the Irrillania Chronicles)
Iambic Rambleameter (Scenes and monologues)
Threads (A heightened language play)
Evidence Room (A play)

About the author:
J.L. Davis is a novelist, playwright, and stage performer
who graduated from Pacific Lutheran University with a
BFA in acting.